Second Edition

Sounds
and
Rhythm

A Pronunciation Course

Second Edition

Sounds
and
Rhythm
A Pronunciation Course

W. D. Sheeler · R. W. Markley

 PRENTICE HALL REGENTS Englewood Cliffs, N.J. 07632

Library of Congress Cataloging-in-Publication Data

Sheeler, Willard De Mont, 1915-
   Sounds & rhythm : a modern pronunciation course / W.D. Sheeler,
R.W. Markley.
    p. cm.
   ISBN 0-13-834003-X
   1. English language–Pronunciation. I. Markley, Rayner W.
II. Title. III. Title: Sounds and rhythm.
PE1137.S37 1991   90-22705
421′.52–dc20   CIP

Editorial/production supervision
  and interior design: **Shari S. Toron**
Acquisitions editor: **Anne Riddick**
Cover designer: **Bruce Kenselaar**
Illustrator: **Len Shalansky**
Prepress buyer: **Ray Keating**
On-press buyer: **Lori Bulwin**

 ©1991, 1981 by Prentice-Hall, Inc.
a Simon & Schuster Company
Englewood Cliffs, New Jersey 07632

Acknowledgements

Rain, rain go away from SONGS FROM THE NURSERY ©1805.

In the Dark, Grown Up, Three Storms, Modern Technology, At the Shore and Inland
© 1990 by Harriet Sheeler.

A Wise Old Owl from THE OXFORD DICTIONARY OF NURSERY RHYMES,
edited by Iona and Peter Opel, Oxford, 1951.

Annabel Lee from THE POEMS OF EDGAR ALLAN POE edited by Thomas
B. Mosher 1901.

A Bird Came Down the Walk from THE POEMS OF EMILY DICKINSON
edited by Martha D. Bianchi and Alfred L. Hampson 1938
by the permission of Little, Brown and Co.

Printed in the United States of America
10 9 8 7 6 5 4 3 2

ISBN 0-13-834003-X

Prentice-Hall International (UK) Limited, *London*
Prentice-Hall of Australia Pty. Limited, *Sydney*
Prentice-Hall Canada Inc., *Toronto*
Prentice-Hall Hispanoamericana, S.A., *Mexico*
Prentice-Hall of India Private Limited, *New Delhi*
Prentice-Hall of Japan, Inc., *Tokyo*
Simon & Schuster Asia Pte. Ltd., *Singapore*
Editora Prentice-Hall do Brasil, Ltda., *Rio de Janeiro*

CONTENTS

Preface ix

UNIT ONE   An Overview of English Pronunciation

Words 2 • Phrases and Sentences 5 • Vowels 9
Consonants 13 • Rhythm 18 • The sound of English 20

UNIT TWO   Basic Stress, Rhythm, and Intonation

Lesson 1 *June, July and August.* Stress of words of one and two syllables 22
Lesson 2 *Carpenter, accountant, engineer, astronaut:* Stress of three-syllable words 23
Lesson 3 *Airplane:* Stress of compound nouns 25
Lesson 4 *Maria's Spanish. She lives in Madrid.* Phrase or sentence stress 27
Lesson 5 *Where's your sister? She's at work.* Falling intonation 28
Lesson 6 *Is that your car? Is it a Volvo?* Rising intonation with yes-no questions 31
Lesson 7 *What's his name? Is it John?* Summary of falling and rising intonation 32
Lesson 8 *I bought a box of candy.* Stress in sentences 34
Lesson 9 *What is your name?* Rhythm 36
Lesson 10 *A hard lesson:* Rhythm—noun phrases 38
Lesson 11 *Money talks.* Using noun phrases as subjects 40
Lesson 12 *Read a good book.* Noun phrases as objects of verbs and prepositions 42

UNIT THREE   Vowels

Lesson 13 *Pit, pet, pat, etc.:* All the vowels 45
Lesson 14 *See the sea.* Length of vowels 47
Lesson 15 *Odd jobs:* The vowel [a] 48
Lesson 16 *Bright lights:* The vowel [ay] 49
Lesson 17 *Sit still.* The vowel [i] 51
Lesson 18 *Green beans:* The vowel [iy] 52
Lesson 19 *Six weeks:* Contrasting [i] with [iy] 53
Lesson 20 *Red pepper:* the vowel [e] 55
Lesson 21 *Late train:* The vowel: [ey] 56
Lesson 22 *A late letter:* Contrasting [e] with [ey] 57
Lesson 23 *A lead lid:* Contrasting [e] with [i] 59
Lesson 24 *He sat on his hat.* The vowel [æ] 60
Lesson 25 *Jan, John, Jane, and Jenny:* Contrasting [æ] with [a], [e], and [ey] 61
Lesson 26 *She came in at ten.* Summary of front vowels 63
Lesson 27 *Strong coffee:* The vowel [ɔ] 64
Lesson 28 *Slow boat:* The vowel [ow] 65
Lesson 29 *Long road:* Contrasting [ɔ] with [ow] 67
Lesson 30 *A small doll:* Contrasting [ɔ] with [a] 68
Lesson 31 *Not much luck:* The vowel [ə] 70
Lesson 32 *Not much water:* Contrasting [ə] with [a], [ɔ], and [æ] 71
Lesson 33 *Good book:* The vowel [u] 74

Lesson 34 *Blue moon:* The vowel [uw]   75
Lesson 35 *Good food:* Contrasting [u] with [uw]   76
Lesson 36 *Bob just bought two old books.* Summary of back vowels   77
Lesson 37 *The boy's toys:* The vowel [oy]   78
Lesson 38 *Down and out:* The vowel [aw]   79
Lesson 39 *A nice loud voice:* Contrasts involving [ay], [oy], [aw]   80
Lesson 40 *Is your car here or there?* Vowels before [r]   81
Lesson 41 *A hurt bird.* The vowel [ᵊr]   82
Lesson 42 *Cora is in the chorus.* The unstressed vowel [ᵊ]   84
Lesson 43 *Older, wiser and richer.* The unstressed vowel [ᵊr]   85
Lesson 44 *Children giggle.* The unstressed syllables [ᵊl] and [ᵊn]   88
Lesson 45 *Very yellow.* The unstressed vowels [iʸ] and [oʷ]   89

UNIT FOUR   Grammar Words and Intonation

Lesson 46 *One, two buckle your shoe.* Counting intonation   92
Lesson 47 *Apples, bananas, and oranges.* Intonation of words in series   94
Lesson 48 *Coffee, tea or milk?* Intonation of alternative questions   95
Lesson 49 *He's coming?* When statements get question intonation   96
Lesson 50 *Where? When?* Question-word questions with rising and falling
                 intonation   97
Lesson 51 *Helen was eighteen.* Stress of numbers   99
Lesson 52 *Eight dollars and sixty-five cents:* Stress of numbers as modifiers   100
Lesson 53 *June third, 1985:* Giving dates and addresses   101
Lesson 54 *Cups and saucers:* Pronunciation of plural nouns   104
Lesson 55 *An arm and a leg.* Pronunciation of a and *an*   106
Lesson 56 *The old and the new:* Pronunciation of *the*   108
Lesson 57 *She laughs and cries.* Pronunciation of third person singular
                 verb form   110
Lesson 58 *You're right: I'm wrong.* Contractions of *am, is, are*   111
Lesson 59 *She isn't here.* The contraction *n't*   113

UNIT FIVE   Consonants

Lesson 60 *Pea, Tea, Key, and so on:* All the consonants   116
Lesson 61 *Look and listen:* The consonant [l]   118
Lesson 62 *Reading and writing:* The consonant [r]   120
Lesson 63 *Left and right:* Consonants [l] and [r]   122
Lesson 64 *Some young men:* Consonants [m], [n], and [ŋ]   123
Lesson 65 *We hear you:* The consonants [y], [w], and [h]   125
Lesson 66 *Too, do, sue, zoo:* Contrasts of voiceless and voiced consonants   128
Lesson 67 *First, thirst, sell, shell.* Contrasts among fricatives   130
Lesson 68 *Day, they, chew, shoe.* Contrasts of stop and fricative Consonants   132
Lesson 69 *Sweet music.* Initial consonants and consonant clusters   136
Lesson 70 *A simple symbol.* Medial consonants and consonant clusters   138
Lesson 71 *Drink your milk.* Final consonants and consonant clusters   141

UNIT SIX   Sentence Stress and Rhythm

Lesson 72   *Sooner or later:* Reduced forms   144
Lesson 73   *Add 'n' subtract:* Reduced forms and rhythm   145
Lesson 74   *Are ya ready?* Subject pronouns   149
Lesson 75   *What's 'er name?* Possessive modifiers   151
Lesson 76   *Help me help them.* Object pronouns   154
Lesson 77   *At the bank at noon.* Prepositional phrases   155
Lesson 78   *Get up, Get down.* Linking of sounds   158
Lesson 79   *English is easy.* Neutral sentence stress   159
Lesson 80   *Burn it up.* Sentence stress (Adjectives and two word verbs)   161
Lesson 81   *He speaks English fluently.* Sentence stress (Adverbs)   164
Lesson 82   *His leg wasn't broken.* Contrastive stress I   166
Lesson 83   *Weaver is an English name.* Contrastive stress II   167
Lesson 84   *Do you want this pen or that one?* Contrastive stress III   169

UNIT SEVEN   Final Practice and Review

172

Teacher Notes and Answer Key

181

Preface

Sounds and Rhythm is designed to help learners of English practice many aspects of English pronunciation. These include the sounds of the language (the vowels and consonants), the rhythm of the language (the patterning of stresses) and the intonation of the language (the musical tone or pitch). All these aspects need to be mastered to some degree in order to communicate intelligibly in English. To get beyond mere intelligibility, further refinement of these aspects will lead to the reduction, if not elimination, of a nonnative accent. While it is not necessary to eliminate a foreign accent totally, most students do feel a sense of satisfaction and accomplishment in coming as close to this goal as they can.

The introductory Overview of English Pronunciation is a listening and familiarization section for beginning students. It is designed solely as an introduction to the salient aspects of English pronunciation. It is not essential that students understand the meaning of all the words and sentences. It is important that the teacher "walk" through the material with the students explaining what the sections are about and translating instructions (as necessary) so that students can participate in the several discrimination exercises scattered throughout the section.

This preliminary section also shows students the whole pronunciation picture before focusing on small pieces of it in subsequent sections. Later, students can return from time to time to regain perspective and understand how the aspects they are practicing fit into an integrated picture.

Few adult students come to courses of this kind without the ability to speak and understand at least a few words and sentences of English and perhaps to read even more. With this in mind, the material in this preliminary unit has been written with elementary vocabulary and is illustrated to help students understand and follow even more of the language.

The lessons of the main text start with Unit 2, Lesson 1. A variety of exercise types generally begin with a short repetition practice and then move to vocabulary or grammar exercises that incorporate the pronunciation point under study. This second step of the lesson allows the students to practice pronunciation while focusing their attention on forming phrases and sentences according to preset patterns. The teacher can monitor and assess the students' control of the pronunciation point and then provide help and practice as indicated.

The final phase in most lessons is an open-ended exercise or discussion that involves examples of the learning point. Here again, the teacher has the opportunity to monitor student control of certain pronunciation points as the students use the language under freer and less controlled situations.

For the most part, the vocabulary and structures used throughout the book are suitable for the elementary level student. But since pronunciation texts are often used for review or remedial work by more advanced students, we have included some exercises of a more challenging nature. For ready identification, these are placed between horizontal bars in the text. Inevitably, students whose experience is more limited will attempt them, and some will be able to do them. We see no reason for discouraging students from reaching as far as their interest and abilities will allow.

Pronunciation differs from person to person, and almost anything can be said in more than one way by using different stresses and intonation. The text represents only one way of saying things. Questions may arise in class when students notice that the teacher's pronunciation differs from that of the text or tapes. If this happens, the teacher should explain that the English-speaking community is used to such differences and adapts to them. The text and tapes represent a kind of American media standard. If the teacher's speech is different from this, he or she should point out differences and have students choose either of these models.

Each lesson title is embedded somewhere in the lesson, and many students will enjoy the challenge of finding it. Often its location is obvious; at other times, it is only by doing an exercise that the title can be found.

The exercises that present the material and provide a model for imitation are very short. If more practice is needed, these can be repeated using different or additional items. Any exercise can be extended, of course, but many can be done and redone by simply changing the items. In Lesson 26 and 36, the bingo words *should* be used again in a different order. Sometimes the student can direct an exercise and choose the item to be used. It is not always necessary to do all of the exercises in a particular lesson. On the other hand, exercise ideas can be taken from one lesson and adapted for use in another lesson. Many of the exercises require preparation beforehand. The students will need prior explanation and preparation before actually doing the exercises in class or using the tapes at home or in a language lab.

It is desirable, but not essential, to use the prerecorded tapes along with the text. When not using the tapes, the teacher can supply the items for repetition and those needed for the exercises. Exercises that are on tape are marked with this symbol 🖸 .

This second edition of *Sounds and Rhythm* has been expanded and refined. A consonant section and more in-depth practice with contrast or emphatic stress have been added, as well as a final section entitled Final Practice and Review. Many other lessons from the original edition have been improved for more effective use in the classroom and for self-study.

Pronunciation Symbols

Vowels in Stressed Syllables

[æ]	at	[ɔ]	all
[a]	odd	[ow]	own
[aw]	out	[oy]	oil
[ay]	eye	[ə]	up
[e]	egg	[ᵊr]	earn
[ey]	aim	[u]	look
[i]	if	[uw]	soon
[iy]	eat		

Consonants

[b]	be	[p]	pie
[ch]	chew	[r]	ray
[d]	do	[s]	so
[f]	few	[sh]	she
[g]	go	[s̶h̶]	Asia
[h]	high	[t]	too
[j]	jay	[th]	think
[k]	key	[t̶h̶]	they
[l]	low	[v]	vow
[m]	my	[w]	way
[n]	no	[y]	you
[ŋ]	king	[z]	zoo

Vowels in Unstressed Syllables

[iʸ]	happy	[ᵊr]	butter
[oʷ]	window	[ᵊl]	apple
[ᵊ]	banana	[ᵊn]	open

4 Stresses: weak   medium

○   ●

Stresses used on individual words

strong   weak   medium

ćelebrate

2 Strong Stresses

strong   phrase or
stress   sentence stress

 ′   ′

Sentence stress
↓

Let's begin to celebrate.

3 Intonation Levels

--- (high) ------

--- (mid) ------

--- (low) ------

Intonation at End of Phrase or Sentence

(falling)   or   (rising)

 UNIT ONE

An Overview of English Pronunciation

For good pronunciation of a language you must speak the sounds of the language (the consonants and vowels) accurately and use the rhythm of the language (the patterns of stress and pitch). In this section of the book, you will listen to all of these features of English pronunciation. You do not need to practice orally at this time, only listen; but you may return to this section later in the course if you wish.

Words

 A. Falling intonation. Listen to the tone of voice fall from high to low.

da da da da da   A B C D E

one two three four five

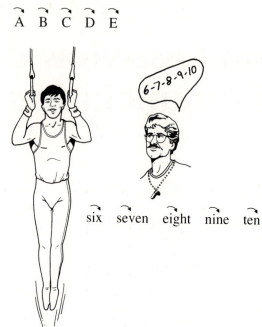

six seven eight nine ten

Tom

Ann

Betty

teacher

Mary

Robert

John

desk   pen   book   pencil   paper

B. Stress. In English, each vowel sound and its nearby consonants form a syllable. Every word is made up of one or more syllables. One syllable of a word is spoken louder or with more force than the other syllable(s). This is called the stressed syllable. Listen to these syllables. Notice that one is louder and a little longer. We use this mark (′) to indicate the stressed syllable.

1. da dá	2. dá da	3. da dá	4. dá da da
da dá	dá da	dá da	da da dá
da dá	dá da	da dá	dá da da

Now listen to this group of syllables.

5. dá da	6. da dá da	7. da dá da	8. dá da
da dá	dá da da	da dá da	da dá da
dá da	dá da da	da da dá	da da dá

C. Listen. Put an X in the column that shows the stress you hear.

	1	2	3	4	5	6
dá da	X					
da dá						

	7	8	9	10	11	12
dá da da						
da dá da	X					

D. Now listen for the stressed syllable. Mark the stressed *da* with (′).

1. dá da	2. da da da	3. da da	4. da da da
5. da da	6. da da da	7. da da	8. da da da
9. da da	10. da da da	11. da da da	12. da da da

E. Listen. These are English words of one, two, and three syllables.

One syllable: gó cóme chíld wánt trý Jóhn

Two syllables: téach·er be·gín wín·dow for·gét léav·ing
　　　　　　　 1　 2　　 1　 2

　　　　　　　 bá·by a·gó réad·ing sís·ter Spán·ish

Three syllables: pro·fés·sor méd·i·cine rá·dio Oc·tó·ber
　　　　　　　　 1　 2　 3　 1　 2　 3

　　　　　　　　 I·tál·ian hós·pi·tal um·bról·la prác·tic·ing

📼 F. Now listen to these words. Do they have one, two, or three syllables? Circle the number of syllables you hear.

1. 1   2 ③   2. 1   2   3   3. 1   2   3
4. 1   2   3   5. 1   2   3   6. 1   2   3
7. 1   2   3   8. 1   2   3   9. 1   2   3
10. 1   2   3   11. 1   2   3   12. 1   2   3

📼 G. Listen for the strong stress in these words.

1. da´   2. da da´   3. da´ da
    ____   _____   _____
    know´   begin´   teacher´
    see´   Japan´   student´
    do´   today´   Mary´

Listen to these two-syllable words.

woman´   window´   machine´   July´   music´   police´   seven´

📼 H. Listen to the words. Put an X in the column that shows that correct stress pattern of each word.

	1	2	3	4	5	6
da´ da Su´ san	X					
da da´ Ber ni´ce						

	7	8	9	10	11	12
da´ da Bur´ ma	X					
da da´ Ja pan´						

📼 I. Mark the strongly stressed syllable of each verb. Use this mark (´).

1. study   stud´·y   5. finish   fin·ish
2. repeat   re·peat   6. pronounce   pro·nounce
3. answer   an·swer   7. explain   ex·plain
4. open   o·pen   8. travel   trav·el

📼 J. Listen for the loud stress in these three-syllable words.

1. da da´ da   2. da´ da da
    _____   _____
    October´   wonderful´
    professor´   beautiful´
    eleven´   president´

K. Now listen to these names. Put an X in the column that shows the correct stress pattern of each name.

	1	2	3	4	5	6
da da da Harriet	X					
da da da Virginia						

Phrases and Sentences

 A. In English, one syllable of a group of words is spoken with more force than the other syllables. This force or loudness is called stress. We use this mark to indicate the loudest stressed syllable: (′).

Listen for the strongest stressed syllable in these *phrases*.

1. the lamp
   two books
   the baby
   a cat

2. on the desk
   on the TV
   on the floor
   in the box

 B. Listen for the strongest stressed syllables in these *sentences*.

This is the living room.
Ann is writing a letter.
The boys are watching a program.
The baby is sleeping on the floor.
The cat is in the box.
He's playing with a ball.

 C. Can you hear the sentence stress? Listen. Then mark the sentence stress.

1. He is reading a book.   2. This is my classroom.
3. She is playing a guitar.   4. He speaks Italian.
5. They are from Thailand.   6. I work in an office.

D. Intonation is the rise and fall of the voice while speaking. If the phrase or sentence stress is on the last syllable, the voice glides down or falls from a high point. Listen.

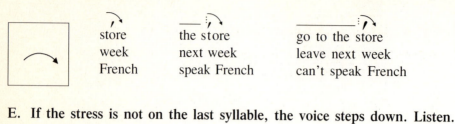

store	the store	go to the store
week	next week	leave next week
French	speak French	can't speak French

E. If the stress is not on the last syllable, the voice steps down. Listen.

drugstore	to the drugstore	go to the drugstore
tomorrow	leave tomorrow	can't leave tomorrow
Spanish	speak Spanish	can speak Spanish

F. Listen to the sentences.

The lamp is on the desk.
The books are on the TV.
The baby is on the floor.
A cat is in the box.

They're in the living room.
Ann is writing a letter.
The baby is playing.
The cat is sleeping.

G. The use of a *question-word* at the beginning of a sentence signals that a question is being asked. Such questions ask for information.

WHO   WHAT   WHEN   WHERE   WHY   HOW

Question word questions generally have falling intonation. Listen.

Where's my book?
Who's that man?
What's her name?
When did you come?

Where's my notebook?
Who's that woman?
What's her telephone number?
When are you leaving?

H. Listen to the statements and questions. Mark the sentence stress with this mark (′).

1. Who's that man?
2. That's Mr. Johnson.
3. What does he do?
4. He teaches English.
5. Where's Ann?
6. She's at her desk.
7. What's she doing?
8. She's writing a letter.

I. Often in this book we use a falling arrow (⌢) at the point of sentence stress to show falling intonation. Listen.

Who's that wŏman?   What does Mr. Jŏhnson do?

What's her năme?

He's a tĕacher.

That's Mary Nŏrris.   He teaches Ĕnglish.

She's a nŭrse.   He's from New Yŏrk.

J. Questions that can be answered by saying *yes* or *no* have *rising intonation*. These words at the beginning of a sentence show that a yes-no question is being asked:

IS   ARE   WAS   WERE

Is the baby sleeping?   Yes, she is.

Is the cat playing with a ball?   Yes.

Are the boys asleep?   No.

K. These words also show that a yes-no question is being asked:

DO   DOES   DID   CAN

In this book, the rising arrow (⌣) is used frequently to mark rising intonation. The arrow is placed at the point of sentence stress. Listen.

Do you know Marc?   Yes.

Does he speak English?   Yes, he does.

Did you live in France?   Yes, I did.

Did you study French?   Yes, I did.

Can you speak it?   Yes, I can.

L. Listen to these yes-no questions with rising intonation. Mark the sentence stress with a rising arrow (⌣).

1. Did you study Spanish?   5. Does Mary live in New York?
2. Can you speak it?   6. Do you know her?
3. Was Ann at her desk?   7. Are you a student?
4. Was she writing letters?   8. Can you hear me?

M. Listen to the different intonations of the two kinds of questions.

What's his \name   Is it James Walker

1. What's his name?   Is it James Walker?
2. Where is my book?   Is it on the table?
3. Who are those boys?   Are they students?
4. When did they come?   Did they come yesterday?
5. How did they come?   Did they come by plane?
6. When can you come?   Can you come tomorrow?

N. Mark the intonation. Listen to the statements and questions. If the tone of voice falls, put an X next to (⌐). If it rises, put an X next to (⌐).

	1	2	3	4	5	6	7	8
⌐	X							
⌐		X						

O. Now listen to these dialogs. Mark the sentence stress of the answers. Use this mark (/).

1. Who's that?   2. Where is your mother?
   That's my sister.   She's in the garage.
3. How do you do?   4. Can you see the plane?
   I'm glad to meet you.   Yes. It's on the runway.

P. Listen to the dialogs. Listen to the stresses and intonation.

Q. Listen to the reading. Listen for the sentence stresses.

I'm Cathy Sasáki.

I live in New Yórk.

I'm márried.

My husband is an Énglish teacher.

We have three chíldren.

I'm a déntist.

I have a small práctice.

I líke my work.

Vowels

A. These are the vowel sounds in English. Listen.

æ	bat–bad	a	cot–cod	ə	tuck–tug
e	bet–bed	ɔ	brought–broad	ᵊr	hurt–heard
i	bit–bid	u	book–could		
ay	bite–bide	aw	house–loud		
ey	bait–bayed	ow	coat–code		
iy	beat–bead	uw	suit–sued		
oy	Hoyt–Floyd				

B. Listen.

æ	
man	that
thank	class

e	
men	friend
desk	chair

i	
is	sit
begin	this

That man.
Thank you.

Ten men.
On the desk.

Sit here.
Let's begin.

C. Listen to the sentences.

　　　　　i　　　i　　i　　　æ
1.　This is our English class.

　　　　　　æ　　i　æ
2.　The class begins at ten.

　　　　æ　æ　　　ii　　　　　e
3.　That's Jan. She's fixing the chair.

　　　　æ　　e　　　　ii　　i　e
4.　That's Ted. He's sitting on his desk.

　　　i　i　æi　　　i　æ
5.　Bill is hanging up his jacket.

　　　　e　　　i　　　e
6.　Ted and Bill are friends.

　　　　　　　i　　　　i　æ
7.　Oh, here's Mr. [mistᵊr] Ash.

　　　　e　　　　　　　　e　　　i
8.　He says, "All right, students. Let's begin."

D. Listen to the words and sentences.

ey	
they	eight
radio	name

e	ey
let	late
tell	tale

i	iy
sit	seat
been	bean

iy	
we	please
read	speak

　　ey　　ey
1.　Jane is baby-sitting tonight.

　　ey　　　　ey　　　ey　ey　ey
2.　Jane's full name is Jane Elaine Ames.

　　iy ey iy
3.　She's eighteen.

　　　　iy　　　iy
1.　Jean is three.

　　　iy iy　　　　　　　　iy
2.　She's reading a magazine.

　　　iy　　　ey iy
3.　Dean is the baby.

　　iy　　iy
4.　He's asleep.

E. Listen to the words and sentences.

ay	
I	like
time	ride

oy	
boy	voice
enjoy	noise

     ay   ay oy
1. Guy is a fine boy.

     iy ay
2. He's nine.

     iy ay   ay
3. He's riding his bicycle.

     oy   ey
1. Joy and Ray are twins.

     ey ey ey   oy
2. They always make a lot of noise.

     ay   ey   oy oy
3. Right now they're playing with some noisy toys.

 F. Listen to the words and sentences.

a	
are	not
water	hot

ɔ	
long	song
talk	call

u	
book	put
cook	good

Is the water hot?

No, it's not.

Who's talking to

Paul?

It's Laura.

Is this your book?

Yes, it's my new

cookbook.

aw			ow			uw	
out	how		no	close		do	you
loud	down		boat	know		moon	who

Dr. Powell, this is   Is her name Jo?   June is a new

Mrs. Brown.   I don't know.   student.

How are you,   She's from Peru.

Mrs. Brown?

G. Listen to the sentences.

     a   a   a
1. What's that?   2. What's that?   3. What's that?
    ow   aw   uw uw
    It's smoke.   It's an owl.   It's a new moon.

    a   ɔ   a   ɔ   a   ɔ
4. What's wrong?   5. What's wrong?   6. What's wrong?
    u   uw uw a   ɔ   uw
    The wood is wet.   The soup is too hot.   He lost his shoe.

H. Listen to this sound.

	ə	
up		come
study		run

The sun is coming up.
She's running for the bus.

The sound [ᵊr], pronounced simply "r," also functions as a vowel.

	ᵊr	
her		were
doctor		nurse

Her sister is a nurse.
Her mother is a doctor.

Consonants

  A. These are the consonant sounds in English. Listen.

y	yes	p	pea	f	fan	s	ice
w	wet	t	ten	v	van	z	eyes
h	hot	k	coat	th	thin	sh	shoe
m	swim	b	bee	**th**	then	**sh**	garage
n	sun	d	den	l	light	ch	cheap
ŋ	swing	g	goat	r	right	j	jeep

  B. Listen to the words and sentences.

	y	
you		year
young		yesterday

	w	
we		wife
were		one

	h	
he		his
home		who
	have	

This is Harry. This is his wife, Wilma.
They are young.
They have one son.
He was one year old yesterday.

C. Listen to the words and phrases.

m	
my	summer
name	

n	
no	in
noon	

ŋ	
sing	bank
long	

my name   at noon   in the morning
the sun and the moon   sing a song

me
knee

gum
gun

sun
sung

Let's swim.
Let's swing.

  D. Listen to the words and word pairs.

p	
pay	open
lamp	up

t	
two	cat
tape	letter

k	
come	back
desk	doctor

b	
be	bed
Bob	baby

d	
do	day
read	did

g	
go	good
egg	again

pen–Ben
cap–cab

town–down
bet–bed

coat–goat
back–bag

  E. Listen to the phrases and sentences.

come back again   do the work   pay the bill   open the door
come to dinner   go to bed   read the letter   play the tape

The lamp is on the desk.
Two books are on the TV.
The baby is sleeping again.
The cat is playing with the ball.
Ann is at her desk.
She is writing to a good friend.

F. Listen to the words and sentences.

f	
face	laugh
phone	if

v	
V[viy]	have
very	of

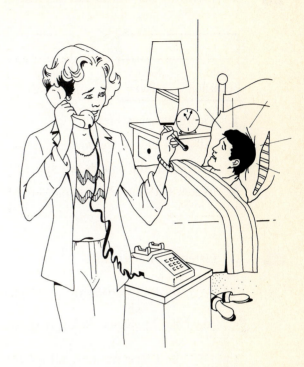

1. It's five after eleven.
2. Mr. Vaughn feels bad.
3. His face is on fire.
4. He has a very high fever.
5. His wife is frightened.
6. She's phoning Dr. Vega now.

 G. Listen to the dialog.

th	
think	three
both	mouth

th	
the	that
weather	brother

th
Joe: Who is that?

Clyde: Where?

th
Joe: Over there.

th　　th　**th**
Clyde: Oh, that's Beth Mathers.

　　　　th
She's an author.

th　　　　　　th
Joe: Who are those two men with her?

th　th　　　　th
Clyde: The thin one is Kenneth.

th　**th**　　　th　　**th**　　th　**th**
The other one is Theodore. They are Beth's brothers.

th
Do you want to meet them?

th　　**th**
Joe: I think so. They look interesting.

H. Listen to the words and sentences.

ch	
child	teach
question	church

ch	j
cheap	jeep

j	
job	large
danger	judge

1. George teaches French.

2. All the children are wearing jeans.

3. She joined the church last June.

4. Watch out! This road is dangerous.

I. Listen to the reading.

      s z   z   j   s   s   sh   sh   z   j   s

Susan is a language student at the University of Chicago. Chicago is a large city

            sh   s z   zs   s   sh   ch   z

on Lake Michigan. Susan is studying Spanish and Portuguese.

          s   sh   s sh   ks   s

Last year she took a trip. First she went to Mexico and to Central America. Then,

      s   sh   z   z   ch   j   z sh s   s

in South America, she visited Venezuela, Chile, Argentina, and Brazil. She speaks

s   sh   ch   z

Spanish and Portuguese very well now.

J. Listen.

s	
see	city
yes	face

s	z
C	Z
ice	eyes

z	
is	zoo
busy	those

     s z   zs   s

1. Susan is sewing her blouse.

      s   z   s   z   s

3. Tess is practicing her music lesson.

             s   z   z z   s z z

2. Mr. [mist°r] Zilmer is using the scissors.

                  s z z   z

4. Mrs. [misiz] Zilmer is reading the

    z

newspaper.

K. Listen.

sh	
shoe	sure
wash	nation

sh	**sh**
nation	Asia
shock	Jacques

sh	
Asia	garage
measure	Parisian

s z sh z sh z   sh z   sh
1. Sid's polishing his shoes. 2. Sharon is watching television.

s   sh s   s   z   sh
3. The cat's washing its face. 4. The cat is in the garage.

L. Listen to the words and sentences.

l	
like	will
little	tall

r	
run	are
hair	rain

1. Do you see those two people?
2. They are walking along the lake.
3. It's raining a little.
4. But they don't care.
5. They are carrying an umbrella.
6. And they are in love.

light	right
long	wrong
pool	poor

In many words, the *r* sound functions as the vowel. Listen.

ᵊr	
her	nurse
father	church

1. Her name is Jennifer.
2. His name is Robert.
3. She is a lawyer.
4. He is a doctor.
5. They were married last Thursday.
6. They were married in that little church on the hill.

Rhythm

A. **Listen to the words. The syllables of words in English have a strong stress or a weak stress. We use this mark [○] to indicate weakly stressed syllables.**

Jane	Johnny	above	president	tomorrow
desk	table	Japan	medicine	professor
now	into	today	bicycle	apartment
see	teacher	again	hospital	piano

B. **Sentences, too, have strong and weak stresses. Listen.**

They are speaking French.   The boys are at the door.

The beat of strong or stressed syllables in an English sentence helps establish a rhythm. Listen to these sentences, which have one, two, or three syllables with strong stress. One stressed syllable in a sentence is a little stronger than the other stressed syllables; this syllable is said to have <u>sentence stress</u>.

One stress:	′	I know him.
		He's a student.
Two stresses:	′ ′	She's learning Spanish.
		She's going to Mexico.
Three stresses:	′ ′ ′	I bought a ticket for Italy.
		I'm leaving for Rome tomorrow.

The stressed syllables help establish a rhythm. There is about the same length of time between stressed syllables in an English sentence. The unstressed syllables are lengthened or shortened to help establish the basic rhythm and timing. This is why English is often called a stress-timed language.

C. **Listen to these sentences. Each takes about the same time to say, although they have different numbers of weakly stressed syllables.**

1. Tom speaks English.
   Helen speaks Spanish.
   Jennifer speaks German.
   Robert is speaking Russian.

2. John is tall.
   Henry is taller.
   Jennifer is the tallest.

D. Listen to these sentences. In each column the sentences have the same number of strong stresses.

1. He práctices médicine.
   He práctices in Páris.　　　　He práctices médicine in Páris.
2. The pláne is from Lóndon.
   The pláne is lánding.　　　　The pláne from Lóndon is lánding.
3. Chicágo is a cíty.
   Chicágo is on Lake Míchigan.　Chicágo is a cíty on Lake Míchigan.
4. I'm léaving for Jápan.
   I'm léaving at nóon.　　　　I'm léaving for Jápan at nóon.
5. She's stúdying Spánish.
   She's stúdying at the univérsity.　She's stúdying Spánish at the univérsity.

E. Mark the number of strongly stressed syllables indicated in each group.

One strong stress:

1. Do you knów him?
2. He's a doc·tor.
3. Is he your friend?
4. Are you leav·ing?

Two strong stresses:

5. Is she smók·ing a cig·a·rétte?
6. He lives in an a·part·ment.
7. Is your um·brel·la bro·ken?
8. His hair is long.
9. Is the ball on the chair?

Three strong stresses:

10. John téach·es chém·is·trý.
11. The plane from Lon·don is land·ing.
12. The ba·by is a·sleep in her bed.
13. She's throw·ing the ball to her friend.
14. The let·ter on the ta·ble is for you.

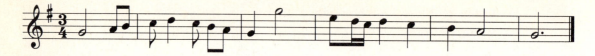

The sound of English

A. Where do the following conversations take place? Match pictures a, b, and c with conversations 1, 2, and 3.

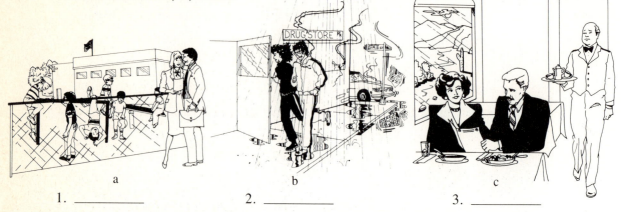

a

b

c

1. _____

2. _____

3. _____

B. Listen for the place name in each sentence.

1. New York
2. New York
3. New York
4. London
5. London
6. London
7. Toronto
8. Toronto
9. Toronto
10. Washington
11. Washington
12. Washington

C. Listen for the place name in each sentence. Some sentences have a place name and others don't. Circle yes if you hear it; circle no if you don't.

1. New York Yes No
2. New York Yes No
3. London Yes No
4. London Yes No
5. Toronto Yes No
6. Toronto Yes No

D. Listen to the native speaker of American English and the nonnative speaker read six sentences. Each sentence will be read twice, first by the native speaker of English, then by the foreign speaker.

E. Now listen to these sentences and decide whether the speaker is a native speaker or a nonnative speaker. Circle N (for native) or F (for foreign).

1. N F
2. N F
3. N F
4. N F
5. N F
6. N F

F. Listen to the conversations. How many people are talking in each conversation? Write the numbers.

a. _____   b. _____   c. _____

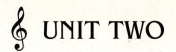 UNIT TWO

Basic Stress, Rhythm, and Intonation

Every English word is stressed on a certain syllable. The strong and weak stresses of the words in phrases and sentences fall into patterns which produce the characteristic rhythm of English. Patterns of pitch accompany sentences, and they distinguish statements from questions. In this section you will practice word stress and sentence stress. Then you will learn falling and rising intonation patterns on simple English sentences. Finally, you will practice the rhythm of English sentences by stressing correctly the noun phrases of a sentence.

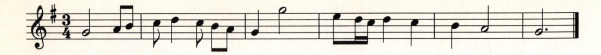

LESSON   1

June, July, and August:
Stress of words of one and two syllables

A. In the two-syllable words, there is a strong stress on one syllable. The other syllable has weak stress. Listen and repeat.

1. June	2. August	3. July
book	paper	begin
pen	pencil	about
road	river	forget

B. Same or different? Listen to 1 through 6. Circle S (*for same*) or D (*for different*) according to the stress pattern of each pair of words.

1. S D   2. S D   3. S D   4. S D   5. S D   6. S D

C. Which type? Listen, and put an X in the column that shows the correct stress pattern of each word.

	1	2	3	4	5	6	7	8
′ ○								
○ ′								

D. Listen. Mark the stress in these words. Mark (′) on the vowel *a, e, i, o,* or *u.*

1. lesson les·son	2. practice prac·tice	3. music mu·sic
4. window win·dow	5. answer an·swer	6. Brazil Bra·zil
7. balloon bal·loon	8. Peru Pe·ru	9. guitar gui·tar

E. The weak or unstressed syllable is often *-er*. Listen and repeat.

teach teacher	buy buyer	run runner
speak speaker	sell seller	drive driver

Now repeat the one-syllable word and add the ending *-er* to form a two-syllable word (work + er = worker).

1. own	2. read	3. print	4. call
5. play	6. swim	7. write	8. send

Talk about these occupations: baker, painter, teacher, writer, farmer, dancer. Tell what each person does. Use the verb (*the form without the* -er *ending*) and the noun. (*A baker bakes bread and cake.*)

F. Two other endings (suffixes) are -*y* and -*ly*. Pronounce these words.

dirt   dirty   safe   safely
noise   noisy   slow   slowly
salt   salty   nice   nicely

Talk about the weather. Include these weather conditions: cloudy, rainy, sunny, windy and the noun that -*y* was added to. (*Is it cloudy this morning? Well, look outside. The weather forecast said there would be clouds all day.*)

G. A number of adverbs and prepositions that begin with *a-* or *be-* have the stress pattern (○/). Listen and repeat the words.

about   again   around   across   above
below   because before   between   behind

Describe the position of things in your room or in the city, using as many of the above words as you can. (*My mother's office is across the street, above the drugstore.*)

LESSON 2

Carpenter, accountant, engineer, astronaut:
Stress of three-syllable words

A. Listen.

1. carpenter   2. accountant
    elephant   important
    hospital   December
    radio   example
    visitor   tomorrow

B. Same or different? Listen to 1 through 6. Circle S (*for same*) or D (*for different*) according to the stress pattern of each pair of words.

1. S ⓓ   2. S D   3. S D   4. S D   5. S D   6. S D

C. **Which type? Listen, and put an X in the column that shows the correct stress pattern of each word.**

	1	2	3	4	5	6
◦◦						
◦◦◦						

D. **Circle the word that has a stress pattern different from that of the other words.**

seventy	animal	eleven
Italy	calendar	Africa

E. **Some words have *medium stress* (•). A syllable that has medium stress is a little stronger and longer than a syllable with weak stress. Listen.**

1. astronaut
    telephone
    alphabet
    exercise
    envelope

2. engineer
    afternoon
    gasoline
    introduce
    entertain

F. **Put an X in the column that shows the correct stress pattern of each word.**

	1	2	3	4	5	6	7	8
◦•								
•◦◦								

G. **Listen to these words. Mark the strong stress over the vowel *a, e, i, o,* or *u.* Use this mark (').**

1. Chevrolet Chev·ro·lét
2. represent rep·re·sent
3. understand un·der·stand
4. photograph pho·to·graph
5. holiday hol·i·day
6. cigarette cig·a·rette

H. **Repeat the names of the occupations and the first and family names in the table.**

	'	' ◦	' ◦ ◦	◦ ' ◦	' ◦ •
Occupations	clerk nurse cook	doctor dentist student	carpenter scientist messenger	mechanic professor reporter	astronaut acrobat diplomat
Women's First Names	Anne May	Sally Janice	Harriet Kimberly	Roberta Anita	Genevieve Josephine
Men's First Names	Tom Fred	Robert Alan	Benjamin Timothy	Arturo Reinaldo	Abraham Constantine
Family Names	Ride Corr	Wilson Fielding	Kennedy Robinson	O'Brien Ortega	Garroway Carradine

Now ask questions or make statements using the occupations and names. With the family names, use Mr., Mrs., Dr., Miss, or Ms.

Examples:
Is Ms. Ride a diplomat? No, she's an astronaut.
Dr. Wilson isn't a professor. He's a dentist.

LESSON   3
Airplane:
Stress of compound nouns

Compound nouns are formed of two words. They are used as a single noun. Compound nouns have several different stress patterns, but characteristically they have strong stress on the first word.

 A. Listen and repeat.

bed + room → bedroom   candy + store → candy store   bus + driver → bus driver

 B. Listen to and repeat these compound nouns.

1. bedroom   2. living room   3. newspaper   4. music teacher
   bookstore   coffee cup   post office   doctor's office
   seashore   swimming suit   eyeglasses   writing paper

 C. Listen to the statement and question. Then answer the question. Use one of the compound nouns above.

1. Tom is sleeping. Where is he? (In the bedroom./He's in the bedroom.)
2. I'm buying some stamps. Where am I?
3. Mary is going to the seashore. What does she need?
4. Jane doesn't see very well. What does she need?
5. John has an earache. Where is he?
6. Ann is buying a textbook. Where is she?

D. **Repeat these compound nouns.**

sports store	barbershop	haircut	wedding ring
card shop	jewelry store	toothpaste	tennis balls
drugstore	clothing store	raincoat	birthday card

Now ask the question "Where are you going?" and reply as in the example. (Where are you going? To the *card shop*. I need a *birthday card*.)

E. **Listen, and mark the strongly stressed syllable in these compounds.**

English class	classroom	homework	textbook
blackboard	English teacher	notebook	tape recorder

Now talk about your school and class. Use the above words or other compound nouns.

F. **Listen to and repeat these compound nouns.**

1. airline	2. plane ticket	3. airline pilot
airplane	air travel	ticket agent
airport		ticket counter

Fill in the compound nouns from above. Then read the paragraphs aloud.

Jack works at an _____. He is a _____. He works for Worldwide Airways. This is an important _____. It has more than 150 large _____.

Jack sells a lot of _____. People prefer _____ today. It is fast and safe.

Jack likes his job, but he has a dream. He wants to be an _____ someday.

G. **Complete the sentences with compound nouns as in the example.**

1. A store that sells candy is a candy store.
2. Water which is good for drinking is called _____.
3. Paper used for wrapping things is called _____.
4. A coat you wear in the rain is a _____.
5. A person who makes sales is a _____.

H. **Now give definitions for each of the compound nouns and say something more about them.**

1. farm equipment   2. fire fighter   3. ice machine   4. cable car

5. auto mechanic   6. bowling ball   7. butter knife   8. history professor
9. racehorse   10. horse race   11. road map

(Farm equipment is equipment used on a farm. Farmers need several kinds of equipment, such as tractors, plows, . . .)

LESSON 4

Maria's Spanish. She lives in Madrid.
Phrase or sentence stress

When two or more words are spoken together, one syllable is always louder or spoken with more force than the others. This is called the *sentence stress*, or the *phrase stress* if only a phrase is involved. We mark it this way: (′).

A. Listen. Then repeat the phrases.

to the store   the tickets   our teacher   my brother
an airline pilot   some candy   going to London   leave tomorrow

B. Listen to the sentences. Then repeat them, paying particular attention to the sentence stress.

I'm going to the store.   Helen Solo is our teacher.

Ted Baker is an airline pilot.   That plane is going to London.

I have the tickets.   Jack is my brother.

Let's make some candy.   I can't leave tomorrow.

C. Listen and repeat. Then mark the sentence stress. Use this mark (′).

1. a. Pam Malik is a teacher.
    b. She's an English teacher.
2. a. I work in an office.
    b. I'm a bookkeeper.
3. a. Maria's Spanish.
    b. She lives in Madrid.
4. a. These are good pens.
    b. They cost fifty cents.
5. a. We're going to London.
    b. We leave tomorrow.
6. a. My brother's an airline pilot.
    b. He's in South America now.

D. **Repeat the words and phrases in the table. Then form sentences.** (*I want a box of candy. The plane tickets are ready.*)

Subject	Verb	Complement
I	want	some apples
This	likes	a box of candy
Mr. James	is	forty dollars
The lamps	are	sick
We	am	on the table
Our airline pilot	speaks	Spanish
The plane tickets	cost	at the drugstore
Maria	works	ready
Dinner	has	ice cream

LESSON   5

Where's your sister? She's at work.

Falling intonation

Statements have falling intonation. Generally the voice begins on a middle level. Then, at the point of sentence stress, it rises and then falls to a lower level and fades away. If the sentence stress is on the last syllable, the tone of voice falls or glides down. If there are syllables after the strong stress, it steps down.

A. Listen and repeat.

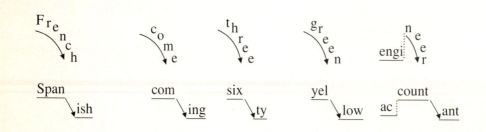

B. Listen and repeat.

He speaks Freⁿc_h

He speaks French.

She's at the store.

She's an engineer.

His suit is blue.

She speaks Span_{ish}

She speaks Spanish.

She's at the drugstore.

He's an accountant.

Her dress is yellow.

C. Question-word questions generally have the same intonation. Listen and repeat.

How is your wi_{fe}

How is your wife?

When did you come?

Where is your son?

Who is that man?

How is your hus_{band}

How is your husband?

When are you leaving?

Where is your daughter?

Who is that woman?

D. Listen. Mark the sentence stress. Then repeat, using falling intonation.

1. I don't understand.
2. Please repeat the question.
3. The lesson is on page six.
4. Where's your sister?
5. She's at work.
6. She works in a hospital.
7. What's your name?
8. Where do you live?
9. What do you do?
10. I'm not a student.
11. I'm an accountant.
12. My brother's an airline pilot.

E. In this book, we will often use this falling arrow (⌢) to indicate falling intonation. The arrow is placed at the point of sentence stress. Listen to and repeat these phrases and sentences.

at the door   in the morning   in front of the bank

Where is he going? To the doctor.   Where is she going? To the dentist.

I'm leaving tomorrow. When are you leaving? Next week.

F. Now listen to the sentences. Then write arrows over the syllable that has the sentence stress.

1. That's my sis·ter.
2. Where is my note·book?
3. She's a trav·el a·gent.
4. What is your ad·dress?
5. My broth·er is a pi·lot.
6. What is your tel·e·phone num·ber?

G. Ask question-word questions or make a statement about the pictures. (*What's his occupation? He's a plumber. What's the plumber doing? He's . . .*)

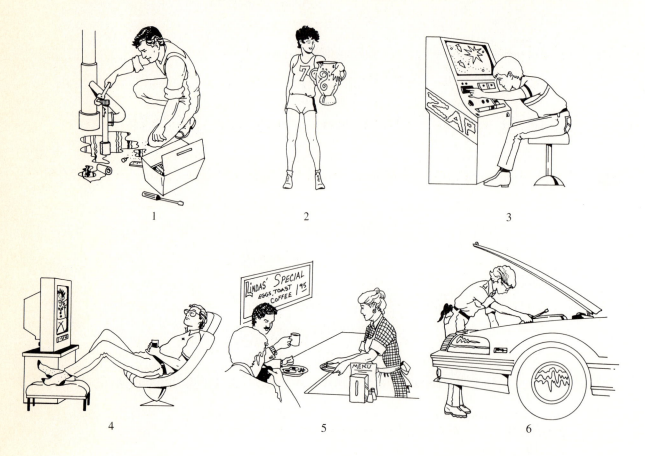

1   2   3

4   5   6

H. Use question-word questions (*who, what, when, where, how*) to ask other students about themselves, members of their families, or friends. Ask name, address, occupation, telephone number, likes, dislikes, hobbies, and so on. The students responding should use full sentences and falling intonation.

Now simulate an interview between an employer or college admissions officer and an applicant. One student prepares questions that he or she asks and a second student responds.

LESSON 6

Is that your car? Is it a Volvo?
Rising intonation with yes-no questions

Yes-no questions are questions that ask for a yes or no answer. This kind of question generally has rising intonation.

 A. Listen and repeat.

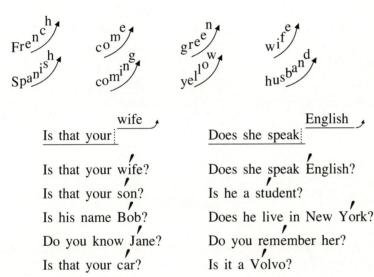

Is that your wife?	Does she speak English?
Is that your son?	Is he a student?
Is his name Bob?	Does he live in New York?
Do you know Jane?	Do you remember her?
Is that your car?	Is it a Volvo?

B. In this book we will often use a little upward arrow (⌣) to indicate rising intonation. The arrow is placed at the point of sentence stress. Listen to these sentences.

Is it late?	Are they sleeping?	Did he explain?
Do you smoke?	Did you study?	Did you forget?
Is it important?	Are you listening?	
Does she remember?	Is she studying?	

C. Listen to the questions. Mark the sentence stress with the upward arrow.

1. Are you a student?
2. Do you speak Italian?
3. Is Ms. Brown your teacher?
4. Do you live in South America?
5. Is your sister a lawyer?
6. Do you play tennis?
7. Are you in class?
8. Do you drive a car?

D. **Ask a yes-no question about each statement.**

1. He isn't a lawyer. (doctor) (Is he a doctor?)
2. John doesn't speak Spanish. (French)
3. She isn't hungry. (thirsty)
4. Helen doesn't like vegetables. (fruit)
5. They aren't studying. (watch TV)
6. My friends don't live in Chicago. (New York)
7. We aren't early. (late)
8. Our son doesn't play tennis. (swim)
9. She isn't a medical doctor. (professor)
10. She doesn't drink tea. (coffee)

E. **Play the game Twenty Questions. One person thinks of something, and others try to determine what it is by asking yes-no questions, no more than twenty. The item may be an animal (*including people, living or dead*), a vegetable (*plants*), or a mineral. Or it can be something made of those things. The word should be one that is familiar to everyone. For example, to guess the word *pig*, students could ask these questions. The student who is thinking of the word responds.**

1. Is it a vegetable? No, it isn't.
2. Is it an animal? Yes.
3. Does it have four legs? Yes.
4. Is it a wild animal? No, it isn't.
5. Is it a farm animal? Yes.
6. Do you ride it? No.
7. Does it eat hay? No, it doesn't.
8. Is it a sheep? No.
9. Is it a pig? Yes, it is.

LESSON   7

What's his name? Is it John?

Summary of falling and rising intonation

A. **Listen. Then repeat the questions. The arrows are placed at the point of sentence stress. They show falling and rising intonation.**

1. What's his name?   Is it John?
2. Who's that girl?   Is it Meredith?
3. Where are my books?   Are they on the table?
4. How's your sister?   Is she all right?
5. When can you come?   Can you come tomorrow?
6. What time is it?   Is it six o'clock yet?

B. Practice these words and phrases which are used in the dialog.

Phrases:	a package	the wrong package	Verbs:	says laughs signs
	some candy	a piece of candy		give/gave send/sent
	some chocolate	some chocolate creams		
	a gift	send a gift	Expressions:	I'm sorry.
	a card	sign a card		Oh, my gosh!

C. Now listen to the dialog. Note especially the arrows that indicate rising and falling intonation.

(Doorbell rings.)

Messenger: Hello. I have a package for Joy Morgan.

Are you Miss Morgan?

Joy: Yes.

Messenger: Sign here, please.

(Joy signs for and takes the package.)

Irene: Who was it?

Joy: Someone sent me a gift.

Irene: Well, open it.

Joy: It's a big box of candy!

Irene: Is it from Chuck?

Joy: No, the card says, "Love, Phil."

Irene: Who's Phil?

Joy: I don't know. Here. Have some candy.

Irene: Mmmmm. It's good!

Joy: Have some more.

Irene: Mmmmm. It *is* good.

(Doorbell rings.)

Joy: Yes?

Messenger: I'm sorry, Miss Morgan.

I gave you the wrong package.

Here. This one is for you.

Joy: The wrong package?

Messenger: Yes. May I have the other one, please?

Joy: *(Laughs.)* Here. *(Laughs again.)* Have a piece of candy.

Messenger: Candy? Oh, my gosh!

Well, *(laughs)* this *is* good candy.

D. Listen to the reading. Then ask questions about it. Ask both question-word and yes-no questions.

Today is an important day for Lucy and Frank Manners. It is their wedding anniversary, their fiftieth. They were married in Scranton, Pennsylvania, in 1940. Frank is now seventy-two, and Lucy is seventy. Frank was an electrician. Lucy was a cashier in Thompson's Drugstore for thirty years.

Their three children are home today. Ted is forty-five. He's a language teacher. He teaches French and Spanish. He's married and has two children, Florence and Billy. He lives in Miami, Florida.

Kimberly is a lawyer. She's single and lives in New York City. She's forty-three.

Foster is an artist. He lives in Los Angeles, California. He's forty and single.

Tonight they are all having a big party. Who is going to cook dinner? Not Lucy Manners! They are all going out to an expensive restaurant!

(Why is today an important day? It's Frank and Lucy's wedding anniversary.

Were they married in New York? No. They were married in Scranton, Pennsylvania.)

LESSON   8
I bought a box of candy.
Stress in sentences

A. We have seen that words of two or more syllables in English have strong stress on one syllable and medium or weak stress on the others. Listen, then repeat these words, paying particular attention to the stresses.

1. at
   desk
   class
   black
   some
   he
   are

2. letter
   under
   study
   writing
   over
   father
   table

3. about
   today

4. studying
   radio

5. professor
   tomorrow

6. afternoon
   understand

B. When words are used in phrases and sentences, some words retain their strong stress. Others do not. Listen for the loud stresses in these sentences. Remember, this mark (′) indicates the sentence stress.

The professor is in cláss. Anne is writing at her désk.

His father is coming tomórrow. Mr. Wilson is wearing a black hát.

C. **Listen to these sentences. Then mark the sentence stress. Use this mark (/).**

1. He put the lamp on the table.
2. Helen is studying English.
3. The doctor looked at the baby.
4. Is English an easy language?
5. Some friends are coming for lunch.
6. Doctors wear white coats.

D. **What kinds of words retain their strong stress in sentences? In general, stressed words are content words: nouns, verbs, adjectives, and adverbs. Listen and repeat the sentences.**

Nouns: Anne, table, desk, professor, book, etc.

Verbs: speak, study, read, writing, studying, etc.

Adjectives: tall, young, new, blue, etc.

Adverbs: today, tomorrow, now, here, etc.

Ánne is sítting at her désk.
(noun) (verb)   (noun)

She is wríting a létter.
     (verb)   (noun)

She's úsing a blúe pén.
     (verb) (adj) (noun)

The páper is whíte.
(noun)   (adj)

She will máil the létter tomórrow.
      (verb)   (noun) (adverb)

E. **Many common words in English do not retain their strong stress when they are used in sentences. We say that their stress is reduced. It becomes either medium or weak stress.**

What kinds of words lose their strong stress in sentences? For the most part, they are short function words (sometimes called grammar words). However, they are some of the most frequently used words in English. Mostly, these are prepositions, pronouns, auxiliaries, articles, and connectors.

Listen to the phrases and sentences and then repeat them.

Prepositions: at, in, of, on,	to	to London	I'm going to London.
about, to, from, etc.	at	at home	Is she at home?
Pronouns: he, his, she, us,	he	he was	He was away then.
them, I, my, etc.	it	mail it	Will you mail it?
Auxiliaries (and *be*): is, are,	is	is studying	She is studying English.
does, will, can, etc.	does	does she	Does she speak it?
Articles: a, an, the, some	a	a book	I need a book.
	some	some money	I need some money.
Connectors: and, but, or	and	and paper	I need pencil and paper.
	or	or tea	Do you want coffee or tea?

F. **Listen carefully to these sentences. Circle the words with weak or medium stress. Then repeat the sentences.**

1. (I) bought (a) box (of) candy.
2. John is my brother.
3. Pam Stokes is a pilot.
4. Is he a doctor?
5. Maria is Spanish.
6. Tom and Alice are teachers.
7. She works in an office.
8. He put the books on the table.

LESSON   9

What is your name?
Rhythm

The juxtaposition of syllables having strong stress with syllables having weak or medium stress creates the characteristic rhythm of English speech. English speech rhythm contrasts with that of many other languages in which each syllable is equally stressed and syllables follow each other at regular intervals. This type of speech rhythm is illustrated below.

English, on the other hand, has a stress-timed speech rhythm. The picture below illustrates the mix of strongly and medium or weakly stressed syllables in English speech.

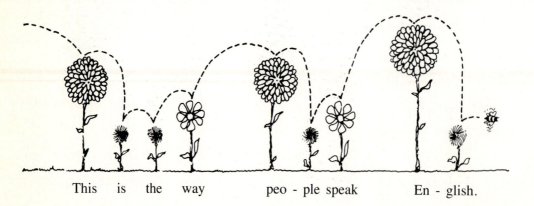

This   is   the   way   peo - ple speak   En - glish.

A. Listen to these groups of sentences. Then repeat them. The sentences in each group have the same stress patterns and are said with falling intonation.

1. Turn to the right.
   Call me tonight.
   Give him the pen.
   Look at the moon.
   What is your name?

2. I went to the movie.
   His home is in Paris.
   They come from Chicago.
   She's mailing the letter.
   He wants to explain it.

3. He's running for the bus.
   His wife is in Peru.
   They moved into their home.
   The furniture is nice.
   She's writing to her son.

B. In English, sentences that have the same number of strongly stressed syllables take about the same length of time to say. A strong syllable along with any nearby weak syllables makes up a unit of time. Each such unit takes about the same time to say because weak syllables are very brief and the strong syllable may be shortened slightly in order to accommodate them. Listen and repeat.

	one time unit	one time unit
write books	write	books
writing books	writing	books
writing some books	writing	some books
writing some booklets	writing	some booklets

C. Listen and repeat. Each group of phrases and sentences has the same basic kind of rhythm. The number of stressed syllables is the same, but each line adds one unstressed syllable.

1. live in Rome
   living in Rome
   living in Paris
   living in Washington

2. go home
   go to school
   go to the store
   go to the office
   go to the hospital
   going to the hospital

3. Marc is French.
   Ann is English.
   Carlos is Spanish.
   Jennifer is German.
   Rosalind is Mexican.
   Meredith is Canadian.

D. Form sentences like the model. Use the same number of strong stresses.

1. You have been doing something for a long time. Now you're tired of it.
   I'm tired of writing.
   write   run   work   wait   look   play

2. You have one hundred dollars. Tell what you'll buy.
   I'll buy a coat.
   coat   radio   sweater   blanket   bicycle   video game

E. Poetry, nursery rhymes and limericks provide some of the clearest examples of the rhythm of English. Listen to the beat of the strongly stressed syllables in these lines. Tap your finger on your desk at each strong syllable.

1. Rain, rain, go away,
   Come again some other day.

   In the Dark

2. Look sharp to the left,
   Now quick to the right.
   A firefly's taking
   Small bites of the night.

   By Harriet Sheeler

   Grown Up

3. Good heavens, Betsy,
   Before I draw a second breath,
   You ask me to call you Elizabeth.

   By Harriet Sheeler

   (Betsy is a nickname for Elizabeth.)

4. There was a young man at the beach
   Who wanted to better his speech.
   He talked to the birds
   And copied their words,
   And now has a marvelous screech.

   By Rayner Markley

LESSON   10

A hard lesson:

Rhythm—noun phrases

A. Determiner + noun. The words *a, an, the,* and *some* are very short and are spoken fast. The articles are spoken with the sound [ə]. Listen carefully. Then repeat.

the book   an apple   a bike   some candy

B. These phrases have the same kind of stress as some words, such as *July*, *tomorrow*, *begin*, and *important*. Listen. Then repeat.

July   tomorrow   begin   example

the book   an apple   a bike   some candy

C. Now repeat the phrases and sentences.

1.   the book.   2.   a bike.

I was reading the book.   She's riding a bike.

3.   an apple.   4.   some candy.

He's eating an apple.   They're making some candy.

D. Adjective + noun. Adjectives are words like *good*, *long*, and *red*. Usually, both the adjective and the noun have strong stress.

good book   tall buildings   wide river   short stories

E. A weakly stressed article often precedes an adjective + noun.

a good book   the tall buildings

He's reading a good book.   We saw the tall buildings.

a hard lesson   some short stories

This is a hard lesson.   She's writing some short stories.

F. Match the adjectives with the nouns to form phrases. (green grass)

Adjectives: green, black, yellow, gray, blue, red | **Nouns:** sky, grass, book, banana, hair, tomato

G. Form noun phrases using determiners, adjectives, and nouns.

a/an	blue	long	little	sweater	boat	shoe
some	black	hot	tall	sheep	cow	horse
	green	cold	nice	sofa	desk	chair
	yellow	old	fast	car	house	bus
	white	new	good	girl	man	baby
	brown	big	fresh	sky	lake	moon
	red	short	comfortable	paper	coffee	water

(a blue sweater, some new shoes, some cold water)

H. Tell about some things you have bought or are planning to buy. Or describe the furnishings of your room or house. Perhaps you have seen some interesting things in the city streets recently. Tell about them. Use as many noun phrases as you can. For example:

(I needed some new clothes. I went shopping downtown a few days ago. I bought some new shoes, a red tie, and a white sweater that I found on sale.)

LESSON   11

Money talks.

Using noun phrases as subjects

A noun phrase may be a single noun, a pronoun, or a noun with modifiers. A noun phrase, whatever its function or position in a sentence, is spoken as a unit and forms a part of the rhythm of the sentence of which it is a part.

A. The underlined words are noun phrases used as sentence subjects. When a noun is present, it generally has strong stress. Listen and repeat.

Babies cry.   People work.   Money talks.   Don smokes.

The door is open.   A plane is landing.

A black cat crossed our path.   Some young boys were playing.

B. Pronouns as subjects may have medium or weak stress. Listen and repeat.

He is smoking.   It is raining.   She's writing.   We're coming.

C. Verbs (*speak, read, writing*) usually have strong stress. Auxiliaries and *be* (*is, are, can, do, was,* etc.) have weak stress. Listen and repeat, paying attention to the verbs.

Strong Stress	Weak Stress
She teaches Spanish.	Dinner is ready.
Don smokes a pipe.	Where are your books?
Your mother is waiting.	I can go tomorrow.
Do you speak French?	She is writing a letter.

D. Form two sentences. Use words from columns 1, 2, and 3. Use a noun as subject in the first sentence. Use a pronoun as the subject in the second sentence.
(*John is writing. He is writing a letter.*)

1	2	3
John	ride	a letter
Mary	teach	tennis
Mrs. Wilson	write	Spanish
Tom and Nancy	read	a bike
Carlos	land	English
Some students	play	on Runway 6
A large plane	study	a short story

E. Look at the picture and form phrases and sentences like the models. Use these words:

Adjectives: young, tall, fat, old, small, big

Nouns: boy, tree, woman, man, lake, boat

Determiners: a, an, the, some

a boy
a young boy
I see a young boy.

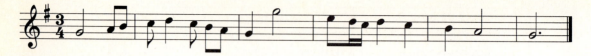

LESSON 12

Read a good book.

Noun phrases as objects of verbs and prepositions

The combination verb + object is commonly spoken as a word group. The object is a noun phrase.

A. Listen to and repeat the phrases. The objects of the verb are underlined.

read books   read a book   read a good book

buy food   buy some food   buy some cheap food

B. Use the words in the table. Form phrases, and questions and answers as in the examples. Use any subject in the questions.

Phrases: a car, some letters
a good car, some new books

Questions and answers: What's Ted doing?
He's writing letters.

or

He's writing a story.

or

He's reading a good book.

Verb	Adjective	Noun
buy	good	car
sell	old	letter
ride	new	book
drive	long	bike
read	hot	story
drink	fast	watch
write	interesting	coffee

C. Listen. This is one common stress pattern of a preposition followed by a noun phrase. Now repeat the phrases several times, saying them as a word group.

to the bank   on the wall   under the lamp   at the door
above the sofa   to the grocery store   near the bus station
on the desk   under the book   to the bus stop   to the office

D. Listen to the sentences, then repeat.

The picture is on the desk. It is under the book.
Tom is going to the bus stop. He's going to the office.

E. Use the words in the table. Form questions and answers as in the model.

Where is Ann going?
To the candy shop.

or

She's going to the candy shop.

Subject	Places	
Ann	bank	post office
Tom and Jane	church	bookstore
Mr. Salim	store	candy shop
Helen	movie	drugstore
He/She/You/They	opera	swimming pool
Miss Todd	park	tennis courts
Fred	lake	seashore

F. Ask where things are in your classroom. Reply as in the model.

Where is the lamp?
On the desk.

or

It's on the desk.

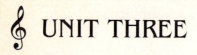 **UNIT THREE**

Vowels

A vowel sound forms the core of every syllable. Vowels are made by shaping the mouth chamber with the tongue and lips. You will learn the seven simple vowels of English and the seven vowels which end with a glide into [y] or [w]. The vowels that are most difficult to distinguish from each other will be contrasted for you. Then you will practice vowels before the sound [r] and vowels that occur in unstressed syllables.

LESSON 13

Pit, pet, pat, etc.
All the vowels

A. These five vowel sounds are similar to vowels in many other languages of the world, but they are not exactly the same. It is important to pronounce them correctly. Listen and repeat.

1. [a] Ah   2. [iy] E   3. [uw] Oo   4. [ey] A   5. [ow] Oh

B. Now repeat these series of sounds.

1. [a] [iy]   2. [a] [ey] [iy]   3. [a] [uw]   4. [a] [ow] [uw]
5. [iy] [a]   6. [iy] [ey] [a]   7. [uw] [a]   8. [uw] [ow] [a]

C. Repeat the sounds once more.

On this facial diagram the five vowels are placed in the position that the tongue is raised in the mouth. With the front vowels, [iy] [ey], the lips are spread, and with the back vowels, [uw] [ow], the lips are rounded.

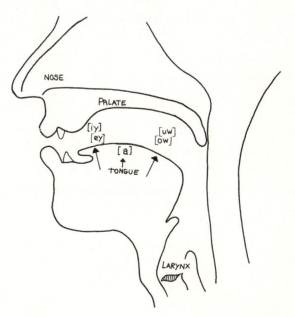

[cassette icon] D. Now read the complete chart of English vowel sounds and the example words.

	Front Vowels	Central	Back Vowels
Tongue High	[iy] [i] key in		[u] [uw] good do
Mid	[ey] [e] day egg	[ə] up	[ow] no
Tongue Low	[æ] at	[a] odd	[ɔ] all
Dipthongs	[aw] now	[ay] my	[oy] boy

One vowel is not located on the chart: [ᵊr] earn.

[cassette icon] E. Say these phrases.

1. on top   2. in the middle   3. at the back   4. along the wall
5. under the bus   6. ahead of Ed   7. good cookies   8. thirty birds

Say these rhyming phrases.

9. One, two,   10. Hello, Joe,   11. How now,
    Buckle my shoe.   What 'd'ya know?   Brown cow?
12. Jump for joy,   13. Way up high   14. A cup of tea
    A baby boy!   In the sky.   For you and me.
                           15. They sailed away
                                For a year and a day.

F. Repeat all the words. Then use some of the words in sentences. Use at least two
   words in each sentence.

1. pit, pet, pat, pot, putt, put, pert, Pete, pate, pout
2. lie, led, lad, laud, lead, laid, loud, lied, Lloyd, load, lewd

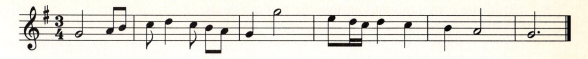

LESSON 14

See the Sea.
The length of vowels

A. Vowel length is affected by the closing consonant. Sounds like [*t*], [*p*], [*k*], and [*s*] (*voiceless consonants*) make the preceding vowel shorter. The words in column a end in voiced consonants; the words in column b end in unvoiced consonants. Listen and repeat.

	a	b		a	b		a	b
1.	did	hit	2.	need	neat	3.	Bill	built
	bed	bet		made	late		well	help
	good	foot		side	right		four	fork
	Bud	but		food	suit		far	March
	had	hat		road	coat		Dan	dance
	Rod	not		loud	out		bang	bank
	broad	brought		bird	Burt		doll	golf

Listen to pairs of words. Circle the one that has the shorter vowel.

4. 1 2   5. 1 2   6. 1 2   7. 1 2   8. 1 2

B. The length of vowels is also affected by stress. Strongly stressed syllables have longer vowels. Say these words and phrases.

1.	see	sea	see the sea	2.	buy	tie	buy a tie
3.	enjoy	toy	enjoy the toy	4.	pay	way	pay your way
5.	hold	gold	hold the gold	6.	lose	shoes	lose your shoes

C. Listen to and repeat the sentence. Then form a sentence like the example.

1. The cat is black.   2. The rat is fat.   3. The shoe is blue.
   (It's a black cat.)   4. The song is long.   5. The day is gray.

6. The pig is big.   7. The wood is good.   8. The ice is nice.

D. Listen to and repeat the groups of words.

Ben	bend	bent		car	card	cart
Bill	build	built		star	large	March

Read the paragraph and answer the two questions.

"Every boy should have a tree house," Bill said to his son. "I had one, and you are going to have one, too."

"I have a hammer. Can I help, too?" Ben asked his dad.

"Of course. But first you have to learn to hammer correctly. Here. Practice on this board. Don't bend the nails!"

The two worked together, and today Ben has his tree house.

1.   What did Bill build?   2.   What did Ben bend?

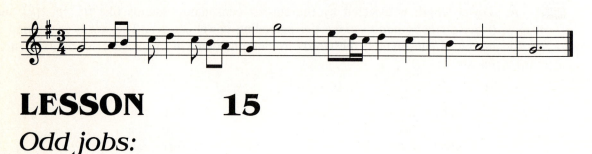

LESSON   15

Odd jobs:

The vowel [a]

For [a], your tongue is in a low position. The jaw and lips are relaxed and open. This is the sound that the doctor tells you to say when he or she wants to look down your throat because your mouth opens the most when you say it.

A. Listen and repeat.

ah	(Say the sound [a], used as an expression of discovery.)
	Ah! That cool breeze feels good.
odd	It's very odd. an odd man an odd job
hot	I feel hot. a hot day It's not hot.

Listen for the sound [a]. Circle the corresponding number if you hear [a] in the word.

1.   2.   3.   4.   5.   6.   7.   8.   9.   10.

B. Repeat the underlined words. Then say the phrases.

1.   a <u>lot</u> of <u>dolls</u>   2.   a <u>box</u> of <u>socks</u>   3.   a <u>drop</u> of <u>water</u>

4.   an <u>odd</u> <u>clock</u>   5.   a <u>modern</u> <u>shop</u>   6.   a <u>hot</u> <u>pot</u>

C. Form noun phrases. Use *a lot of* + plural noun (*a lot of bottles*).

1.   bottle   2.   box   3.   clock   4.   dollar   5.   drop
6.   job   7.   pot   8.   watch

D. Form two sentences. Use _not_. (_It's a baby. It's not a doll._)

1. baby/doll	2. clock/watch	3. rock/log	4. top/bottom
5. box/bottle	6. school/shop	7. toad/frog	8. mop/broom
9. pan/pot	10. sock/stocking	11. bomb/rock	12. pancake/waffle

E. Form questions and answers. (_What does Bob want? He wants a watch._)

1. Bob	2. Mrs. Coggins	a doll	some socks
3. Connie	4. Ronnie	a watch	some odd jobs
5. Mr. Dodge	6. Rosalind	a new clock	some stockings
7. John	8. Tom	a bottle of water	some water

F. Form sentences. Use a past verb and a plural noun. (_He dropped a lot of boxes._)

drop   borrow   rob   watch   get

G. Tell a story about a robbery. Use some of the given words. You will tell your story to the class, and other students will listen and write numbers 1, 2, 3, and so on, to show the order in which the words are used in the story.

___ box (noun)	___ dollar (noun)	___ rob (verb)	___ top (noun)
___ clock (noun)	___ job (noun)	___ shop (verb, noun)	___ watch (verb, noun)
___ doctor (noun)	___ knock (verb)	___ stop (verb, noun)	

LESSON   16

Bright lights:
The vowel [ay]

For [**ay**], your tongue begins in a low position with the jaw relaxed and open. Then the front of the tongue rises, and the lips spread.

A. Listen and repeat.

eye	(Say the sound [**ay**], which is also a complete word.)		
hide	Run and hide.	Hide the eggs.	Hide your eyes.
write	Read and write.	Write the word.	Write it or type it.

Listen for the sound [ay]. Circle the corresponding number if you hear [ay] in the word.

1.   2.   3.   4.   5.   6.   7.   8.   9.   10.

B. Repeat the underlined words. Then say the phrase.

1. a <u>white</u> <u>line</u>   2. a <u>dry</u> <u>knife</u>   3. a <u>bright</u> <u>sky</u>
4. a <u>nice</u> <u>wife</u>   5. a <u>high</u> <u>price</u>   6. a <u>wide</u> <u>tie</u>

C. Form sentences. (*I like the bike. It's quite light*.)

1. bike/light   2. highway/wide   3. child/nice
4. light/bright   5. rice/white   6. site/high

D. Form sentences. (*He's riding his bike. I'll ride my bike, too*.)

1. ride/bike   2. fly/kite   3. clean/typewriter
4. sign/name   5. hide/eyes

E. Tell a short story to the class. Use as many of the given words as you can. The other students will listen for the words and write 1, 2, 3, and so on, to show the order in which you used them in the story.

____ bright (adj.)	____ cry (verb)	____ frighten (verb)	____ lightning (noun)
____ night (noun)	____ sky (noun)	____ child (noun)	____ eye (noun)
____ hide (verb)	____ like (verb)	____ shine (verb)	____ time (noun)

F. Say these words. Then use each group in a sentence.

1. eyes/wide/fright   2. drive/right/side/highway   3. nine/night

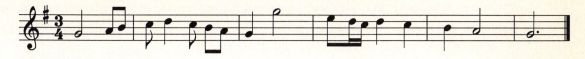

LESSON   17

Sit still.
The vowel [i]

For [**i**], your lips are spread, and the front of your tongue is raised.

A. Listen and repeat.

[**i**]   (Say the sound [**i**].)
did   I certainly did.   Did you work?   I did the dishes.
sit   Will you sit?   Sit down.   Please sit still.

Listen for the sound [i]. Circle the corresponding number if you hear [i] in the word.

1.   2.   3.   4.   5.   6.   7.   8.   9.   10.

B. Repeat the phrases. Notice the function (*grammar*) words that have the sound [i].

1. this building   2. Is he swimming?   3. in the middle
4. his finger   5. Did he swim?   6. with your finger
7. a little English   8. Will he swim?

C. Form sentences like this: Bill's sitting with his sister.

1. Bill/his sister   2. Jim/Chris   3. Dick/Kim   4. Mr. King/Miss Fisher

Form two sentences. (*I have a fish. She has six fish.*)

5. fish   6. pickle   7. big stick   8. hurt finger

D. Choose a group of words and finish each sentence like the example. (*With our hamburgers we had pickles and potato chips.*)

1. With our hamburgers we had _____.   fish, chicken

2. For lunch they served _____.   fish, pickles

3. On the farm they had _____.   pickles, potato chips

4. At the store we got _____.   pigs, chickens

E. Form sentences. Use a name as the subject, the past form of an irregular verb, and a noun. (*Chris hid the gift. Bill slid down the hill.*)

| Chris | Jim | bite | light | gift | kitchen | lip | pit |
| Bill | Sid | hide | slide | hill | lid | nickel | cigarette |

F. Ask about the size of things. Use *big* and *little*. (*Do you live in a big house? Yes, I do./ No, it's little.*)

Ask about the thickness of things. Use *thick* and *thin*. Give approximate thickness in inches (1 inch = |_____|) when possible. One inch equals 4.1516 cm. (*Is your dictionary thick? No, it's a thin one./Yes, it's about six inches thick.*)

G. Say the pairs of words. Note that the vowels [*ay*] and [*i*] occur in each pair. Then use the words to complete the sentences orally.

vines   vineyard   1. Several _____ were taken from the _____.

five   fifth   2. There are _____ new students in the _____ grade.

dining   dinner   3. We'll serve _____ in the _____ room.

child   children   4. Out of fifty _____ only one _____ passed the test.

wise   wisdom   5. The _____ person through excess of _____ is made a fool.

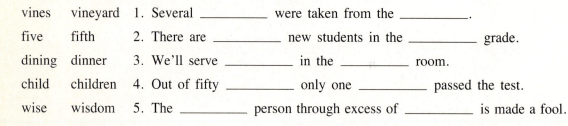

LESSON   18

Green beans:
The vowel [iy]

For [**iy**], your lips are spread, and the front of your tongue is raised. Then the lips spread more, and the tongue moves slightly higher. You can smile easily when making this sound, so a photographer will often tell you to say "cheese."

A. **Listen and repeat.**

E	(Say the sound [**iy**], which is also the name of a letter.)		
read	Learn to read.	Read the sign.	Read aloud, please.
eat	Time to eat.	Eat your food.	Eat the green beans.

Listen for the sound [iy]. Circle the corresponding number if you hear [iy] in the word.

1.   2.   3.   4.   5.   6.   7.   8.   9.   10

B. Form sentences. Use names, verbs, and noun objects from the list. (*Jean cleans her teeth every morning.*)

Jean	Neal		cleans	eats	speaks		teeth	leaves	cheese
Pete	Steve		keeps	feeds	needs		sheep	meat	Greek

C. Form a sentence from each group of words. (*We need some clean sheets.*)

1. clean, need, sheets, some, we
2. in, me, please, see, three, weeks
3. evening, he's, in, leaving, the
4. cream, Eva, her, in, likes, tea
5. machines, never, seen, she's, these
6. a, eat, lot, of, pizza, teenagers

LESSON 19

Six weeks:

Contrasting [i] with [iy]

A. Listen and repeat.

seed	Sid	Sid needs more seed.	The seed belongs to Sid.
beans	bins	some bins of beans	the beans in the bins
seat	sit	Please sit in this seat.	Which seat did he sit in?

Listen to pairs of words. Are they the same word, or are their vowels different? Circle S or D.

1. S D   2. S D   3. S D
4. S D   5. S D   6. S D

Listen to each word. Circle the vowel symbol which you hear.

7. [i] [iy]   8. [i] [iy]   9. [i] [iy]
10. [i] [iy]   11. [i] [iy]   12. [i] [iy]

B. Say the words in each table. Then say the given phrases and form some new ones.

Modifiers	Adjectives		Nouns	
this	big	sick	children	fish
six	little	rich	women	finger
these	cheap	clean	piece	cheese
three	real	green	week	people

Prepositions	Verbs		Nouns	
in	kick	bring	ship	chicken
with	drink	hit	river	English
between	see	speak	tree	tea
	eat	teach	street	knee

Mod. + Noun

these women

six weeks

_____

_____

Adj. + Noun

big people

green fish

_____

_____

Prep. + Noun

in the tree

with a ship

_____

_____

Verb + Noun

see a chicken

hit my knee

_____

_____

C. Listen and repeat. Then choose the correct answer, a or b.

1. sheep/ship

   Is that _____ heavy?

   a. Yes, it's 200 pounds.

   b. Yes, it's 40,000 tons.

2. leave/live

   When did they _____ there?

   a. From 1976 to 1981.

   b. In the afternoon.

3. feel/fill

   Did she _____ the bottle?

   a. Yes, she put warm milk in it.

   b. Yes, it was warm.

4. heat/hit

   Did Mr. Gale _____ the ice?

   a. Yes, and it broke.

   b. Yes, and it melted.

D. Form sentences. Use both words of each pair in each sentence.

1. he's/his   2. fit/feet   3. beat/bit   4. did/deed   5. hill/heel

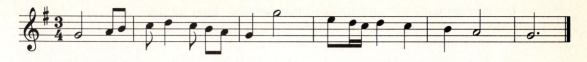

LESSON 20

Red pepper:
The vowel [e]

For [e], your lips are spread a little, and the front of your tongue is raised a little.

A. Listen and repeat.

[e]	(Say the sound [e].)		
bed	Go to bed.	The bed is soft.	I'll get to bed.
bet	I don't bet.	Don't bet your money.	We never bet.

Listen for the sound [e]. Circle the corresponding number if you hear [e] in the word.

1.   2.   3.   4.   5.   6.   7.   8.   9.   10.

Repeat the noun phrases.

many pens	many friends	every belt	every desk
many letters	many steps	every egg	every bed

B.   Form noun phrases. Use an adjective and a singular or plural noun. (messy desk)

best	messy	ten		bed	friend	pepper
heavy	red	wet		desk	letter	step

C.   Form questions and answers like the example. (When will you *send the check?* I'll *get paid on Wednesday*. I'll *send it* then.)

1. send the check/get paid on Wednesday
2. tell your friend/be in Texas in September
3. check the bedroom window/get up at ten
4. sell your chemistry textbook/take the final test on Wednesday

D.   Form questions with *ever*. Form answers with *never* or *seldom*. (*Do you ever get up at ten? No, I never/seldom do.*)

1. get up at ten
2. send a letter to Denmark
3. get egg on your shirt
4. forget your belt
5. tell lies
6. step on anyone's foot

E. Answer with the past tense of the irregular verb. (*I felt well.*)

1. How did you feel? (well)
2. Who did he meet? (friend)
3. How did you go? (jet)
4. What did she read? (letter)
5. When did you leave? (eleven)
6. Where did she fall? (step)
7. Where did you sleep? (bed)
8. What did he feed? (pet)
9. What did he say? (hello)
10. How many pens did it hold? (ten)
11. What did he mean? (farewell)
12. How much did she bleed? (a lot)
13. Where did she keep her sweater? (the second drawer)
14. Where did Henderson lead them? (French restaurant)
15. Where did the baby creep? (the bedroom)

LESSON   21

Late train:

The vowel [ey]

For [**ey**], your lips are spread a little, and the front of your tongue is raised a little. Then the lips spread more as the tongue moves higher.

A. Listen and repeat.

A	(Say the sound [ey], which is also the name of a letter.)		
name	What's your name?	Name the baby.	a famous name
late	You're late.	late today	a late train

Listen for the sound [ey]. Circle the corresponding number if you hear [ey] in the word.

1.   2.   3.   4.   5.   6.   7.   8.   9.   10.

B. Form phrases with *the same* and these nouns. (*the same plane*)

| plane | cake | tape | paper | game | station | baby |
| place | lake | day | table | name | radio | |

Now use the phrases in forming sentences. (*John and Henry are on the same plane.*)

C. Form sentences that use the adjectives *famous* and *strange* with nouns in the list in Part B. (*Rockefeller is a famous name.*) Now form sentences that use one of these six verbs and a noun object from the list in Part B above. (*I know how to bake that kind of cake.*)

bake	pay for	wait for
change	play	paint

D. Form sentences. Use the names, the past tense of the verbs, and noun objects from the list. (*Dave gave them a raise in pay.*)

Dave	Jane	become	eat	give	grapes	table	baseball player
Gail	Wade	come	forgive	lie	mistake	train	raise in pay

LESSON   22

A late letter:
Contrasting [e] with [ey]

A. Listen and repeat.

edge	age	the edge of the table	the age of the car
tell	tale	He always tells tales.	I have a tale to tell.
get	gate	Get your ticket at the gate.	The gate opens at ten.

Listen to pairs of words. Are they the same word, or are their vowels different? Circle S or D.

1. S D   2. S D   3. S D   4. S D   5. S D   6. S D

Listen to each word. Circle the vowel symbol which you hear.

7. [e] [ey]   8. [e] [ey]   9. [e] [ey]
10. [e] [ey]   11. [e] [ey]   12. [e] [ey]

B. Say the words in the table. Then say the given phrases and form some new ones.

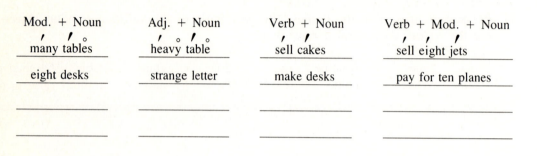

Modifiers	Adjectives		Verbs		Nouns		
many	red	heavy	get	send	egg	desk	pepper
every	wet	fresh	set	sell	jet	friend	letter
ten	late	strange	make	pay for	cake	mail	table
eight	famous	brave	take	wait for	plane	name	player

Mod. + Noun

many tables

eight desks

Adj. + Noun

heavy table

strange letter

Verb + Noun

sell cakes

make desks

Verb + Mod. + Noun

sell eight jets

pay for ten planes

C. Form sentences with the verbs *get* or *stay* and the prepositions *ahead of*, *next to*, and *away from*. (Stay away from the fire.)

D. Listen and repeat. Then choose the correct answer, a or b.

1. sail/sell

   Did you _____ the boat?

   a. No, it was stormy.

   b. No, I'll keep it.

2. taste/test

   Did you _____ this?

   a. Yes, it was delicious.

   b. Yes, it passed.

3. pain/pen

   Do you have a ____?

   a. Yes, in my leg.

   b. Yes, do you want it?

4. chase/chess

   Are they playing ____?

   a. No, they don't like thinking games.

   b. No, they can't run in here.

LESSON 23

A lead lid:

Contrasting [e] with [i]

A. Listen and repeat.

lead	lid	The lid is made of lead.
ten	tin	Ten tin cans fell off the shelf.
bet	bit	She bet quite a bit of money.
spell	spill	How do you spell *spill*?

Listen and repeat. Then circle the word that you heard in the sentence.

1. lead   lid   The _____ fell on my toe.
2. pens   pins   How much are the _____?
3. mess   miss   You won't _____ the blanket.
4. spell   spill   It's easy to _____ soup.

B. Repeat the sentence. Then substitute names from the list.

It's for *them*, not for *him*.

Names: Betty, Cliff, Ted, Chris, Jim, Sid, Jenny, Mel, Jill

C. Complete the phrases and sentences.

little	get	men	building	rest	drink
red	give	women	minute	pen	cigarette

1. in a _____(noun)_____
3. a nice _____(adj.)_____ _____(noun)_____

2. the _____(noun)_____ of the _____(noun)_____
4. _____(verb)_____ me a _____(noun)_____ .

D. Form a sentence with either *till then* or *since then* to follow each sentence. (*My last test is on Wednesday. I can't go anywhere till then.*)

1. The baby is due next week.
2. He broke his arm in the accident.
3. He lost everything in the fire.
4. Her next paycheck will come May 1.

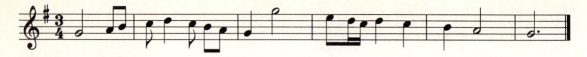

LESSON   24

He sat on his hat.
The vowel [æ]

For [æ], your jaw is open wide, your lips are spread, and the front of your tongue is slightly raised.

A. Listen and repeat.

agh	(Say the sound [æ], used as an expression of displeasure.)
	Agh, now I got my hands all dirty.
add	I can add. Add these numbers. Add them fast.
hat	my hat my hat and coat That's my hat.

Listen for the sound [æ]. Circle the corresponding number if you hear [æ] in the word.

1.   2.   3.   4.   5.   6.   7.   8.   9.   10.

B. The sound [æ] may sound different before different consonants (depending on the speaker's dialect). Listen and repeat.

1.	at add	2.	match half	3.	Jack likes jazz.
4.	cap cab	5.	bag cash	6.	a bag or a can
7.	back bath	8.	hang pass	9.	plants and animals

C. Form phrases or sentences

1.   that + noun (that man)
2.   a + adj. + noun (a bad map)
3.   name + is + adj. (Sam is fat.)
4.   verb + the + noun (Pass the taxi.)

Nouns		Adjectives	Names	Verbs
apple	hat	angry	Jack	carry
bag	man	bad	Madeline	hang
cat	map	black	Pat	laugh at
class	taxi	fast	Sally	pass
		fat	Sam	
		happy		

D. Answer with full sentences. Use the past tense of the verb.

Where did he sit? (He sat on his hat./He sat with Sally.)

1. What did she ring?
2. What did they sink?
3. Who did he run from?
4. What did they sing?
5. What did you begin?
6. How far did she swim?

LESSON 25

Jan, John, Jane, and Jenny:
Contrasting [æ] with [a], [e], and [ey]

A. The sounds [æ] and [a]. Listen and repeat.

add	odd	Add the odd numbers.	They are odd numbers to add.
Jan	John	Jan and John are twins.	John looks like Jan.
hat	hot	a hat for hot weather	It's hot; I'll wear a hat.

Listen to pairs of words. Do they both have the vowel [æ], do they both have [a], or do they have different vowels? Circle [æ], [a], or both [æ] and [a].

1. [æ] [a]
2. [æ] [a]
3. [æ] [a]
4. [æ] [a]
5. [æ] [a]
6. [æ] [a]

B. Tell what color hair students in the class have (or famous people that you know). Use *black*, *blond*, and *red*. (*Maria has black hair.*)

C. Tell whether you "have a friend in" or "want to go to" any of these places. (*I have a friend in Miami.*)

| Miami | Montana | Kansas | Athens | Taiwan | Panama |
| Seattle | Hawaii | Alabama | Moscow | Japan | Guatemala |

D. Repeat the names, verbs, and nouns. Then form sentences using *can't*. (*Matt can't copy the answer.*)

Matt	Pam	catch	stop	cab	clock
Jack	Sally	have	wrap	doll	answer
John	Bonnie	copy	pass	job	exam

E. The sounds [æ] and [e]. Listen and repeat.

had	head	Jenny had a cut on her head.	Her head had blood on it.
pan	pen	Where's the frying pan?	Lend me your pen.
batter	better	This batter is better.	It's better batter.

F. Do you hear the sound [æ] or the sound [e] in these names? Circle [æ] or [e].

1. [æ] [e]   2. [æ] [e]   3. [æ] [e]   4. [æ] [e]
5. [æ] [e]   6. [æ] [e]   7. [æ] [e]   8. [æ] [e]

G. Listen and repeat. Then circle the word that you heard in the sentence.

1. man   men   The new _____ will start work today.
2. pat   pet   You can _____ the horse's nose gently.
3. gas   guess   That was the wrong _____.
4. laughed left   She looked at them and _____ right away.

H. The sounds [æ] and [ey]. Listen and repeat.

mad	maid	I'm mad at the maid.	The maid is mad, too.
Jan	Jane	Jane takes care of Jan.	Jan is Jane's daughter.
cat	Kate	Kate has a nice cat.	The cat belongs to Kate.

I. Listen and repeat. Then circle the correct answer, a or b.

1. tap/tape

   Listen. Do you hear a ____?

   a. Yes, it's rain on the window.

   b. Yes, it's an English lesson.

2. pan/pain

   How did you get the ____?

   a. I probably ate something.

   b. I found it on sale.

3. rack/rake

   What's a ____ for?

   a. We get stones out of the garden.

   b. We hang hats on it.

J. Listen. Which underlined word has [æ] and which has [ey]? Write 1 (for [æ]) and 2 (for [ey]) over each underlined word.

1. Georgia speaks Spanish, but she doesn't come from Spain.
2. There's not much shade at noontime, and things have smaller shadows then.
3. Some people bathe in a warm bath every day.
4. When people are no longer sane, we say they have lost their sanity.

LESSON 26

She came in at ten.
Summary of front vowels

A. Listen to each group of words read in the order written. Then listen to them read in a different order. Write numbers 1 through 5 to show the order that you hear them.

1. beat ____   bit ____
   bait ____   bet ____
        bat ____

2. lead ____   lid ____
   laid ____   led ____
        lad ____

3. dean ____   din ____
   Dane ____   den ____
        Dan ____

Form sentences. Use two of the words above in each sentence. (*He beat his horse, and it bit him.*)

B. Form a sentence from each group of words.

1. she   in
   came   ten
     at

2. Greek his
   hates Ted
     class

3. each   six
   place beds
     has

4. sweet still
   bakes bread
     Ann

C. Play bingo. Choose one of these two cards. Listen to the words. Mark each word as you hear it. When a row (vertical, horizontal, or diagonal) is marked, you are a winner.

[i]	[iy]	[e]	[ey]	[æ]
lip	need	best	mail	mad
fit	seat	ten	cave	fat
win	feel	FREE	wait	map
pig	be	let	bake	hand
did	mean	red	name	match

[i]	[iy]	[e]	[ey]	[æ]
bill	piece	head	main	match
lip	seat	best	cave	mad
fit	need	FREE	mail	fat
win	be	well	bake	map
pig	feel	let	wait	hand

D. Listen to this tongue twister. Then explain the meaning in your own words.

Betty bought a bit of butter.
"But," said she, "this butter is bitter.
If I put it in my batter,
It will make my batter bitter."
So she bought some better butter,
Better than the bitter butter,
And it made her bitter batter better.

LESSON 27

Strong coffee:
The vowel [ɔ]

For [ɔ], your jaw is open wide, lips are rounded, and the back of your tongue is slightly raised.

A. Listen and repeat.

awe	(Say the sound [ɔ], which is also a complete word.)		
broad	The river's broad.	broad river	We live on Broad Street.
fought	The boys fought.	They fought hard.	They all fought.

Listen for the sound [ɔ]. Circle the corresponding number if you hear [ɔ] in the word.

1.   2.   3.   4.   5.   6.   7.   8.   9.   10

B. Say the words in the table. Then say the given phrases and form some new ones.

Adjectives	Verbs	Nouns	
awful	call	ball	lawn
long	cross	boss	song
small	draw	coffee	talk
strong	walk	law	wall

Adj. + Noun
an awful law
a long song
_____
_____

Verb + Noun or Prep. Phrase
call the boss
walk on the lawn
_____
_____

C. Form prepositional phrases. Use *across*, *along*, and *off*. Use any suitable noun, such as *lawn*, *river*, or *street* (*along the wall*, *off the street*).

D. Read Walter's plans for the summer. Then imagine that the summer is over and he is telling a friend about what he did. Use the past tense.

> I'm going to stay at a ranch in North Dakota this summer. I'll buy some outdoor clothes. A cowboy will teach me many things there. I'll see some Indians. I'll catch a lot of fish. I'll fight a bear and bring back a bearskin. Maybe I'll think about home at first, but I'll soon lose my homesickness.
>
> (I stayed at a ranch in . . .)

LESSON 28

Slow boat:
The vowel [ow]

For [**ow**], your lips are rounded a little, and the back of your tongue is raised a little. Then the lips round more, and the tongue moves higher.

A. Listen and repeat.

oh	(Say the sound [ow], used as an expression of surprise.)		
	Oh! I didn't know I needed my driver's license.		
road	on the road	The road turns.	those roads
boat	Take a boat.	The boat floats.	a slow boat

Listen for the sound [ow]. Circle the corresponding number if you hear [ow] in the word.

1.   2.   3.   4.   5.   6.   7.   8.   9.   10.

B. Form two sentences like the examples. In the second, use an adjective which has the sound [ow] and is opposite in meaning to the first one. (*These boats are fast. Those are slow.*)

1. boats/fast
2. roads/closed
3. sofas/new
4. bowls/hot
5. windows/high

C. Form sentences. Use the verbs and nouns in the list. Use the past tense. (*The rope broke./The truck broke the rope.*)

| break | sell | steal | wake | | boat | gold | motorcycle | Polish |
| ride | speak | tell | write | | soldier | joke | poem | rope |

D. Name these things. All of them have the sound [ow]. Then make sentences about them. (*I won't forget my coat.*)

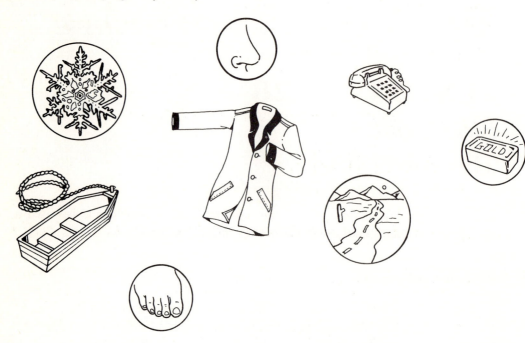

LESSON 29

Long road:

Contrasting [ɔ] with [ow]

A. Listen and repeat.

so	saw (cut)	Did he saw the wood?	I think so.
bowl	ball	I bowl with that ball.	It's a bowling ball.
coat	caught	My coat caught on a nail.	The nail caught my coat.

Listen to pairs of words. Are they the same word or are their vowels different? Circle S or D.

1. S D   2. S D   3. S D
4. S D   5. S D   6. S D

Listen to each word. Circle the symbol of the vowel sound that you hear.

7. [ɔ] [ow]   8. [ɔ] [ow]
9. [ɔ] [ow]   10. [ɔ] [ow]
11. [ɔ] [ow]   12. [ɔ] [ow]

B. Say the words in the table. Then say the given phrases and form some new ones.

Adjectives		Verbs		Nouns		
long	soft	call	fall	ball	lawn	talk
small	tall	draw	walk	boss	salt	wall
cold	old	go	hold	boat	home	road
low	slow	know	throw	bowl	phone	rope

Adj. + Noun: a lóng bóat, a lów wáll, _____, _____

Verb + Noun or Prep. Phrase: wálk on the róad, cáll your bóss, _____, _____

C. Form noun phrases. Use *all* or *both* and a noun from the above table (*all of the ropes, both of the bosses*). Use the phrases in sentences.

D. Form sentences. Use *don't* (or *won't*) and *ought to.* (*I don't have a phone, but I ought to. They won't stop smoking, but they ought to.*)

E. Answer with the past tense of the verb.

1. Did you ever *lose* anything valuable?
2. Did you ever *break* anything valuable?
3. Did you ever *buy* anything over $5,000?
4. Did you ever *write* a long letter?
5. Did you ever *sell* something that wasn't yours?
6. Did you ever *bring* something to class that the teacher didn't like?

F. Listen and repeat. Then choose the correct answer, a or b.

1. call/coal

   When was the ____ made?

   a. Just last week.

   b. Millions of years ago.

2. lawn/loan

   How big is their ____?

   a. It's over $20,000.

   b. It's almost an acre.

3. cost/coast

   Is the ____ all right?

   a. No, it's too expensive.

   b. No, there are too many rocks.

4. bald/bold

   Is John very ____?

   a. No, he's afraid of mice.

   b. No, he has lots of hair.

LESSON   30

A small doll:
Contrasting [ɔ] with [a]

Some speakers of American English do not make the distinction between these two vowel sounds.

A. Listen and repeat.

caught	cot	I slept on a cot.	I caught cold.
dawn	Don	Don was up at dawn.	The dawn seemed cold.
awed	odd	The water tasted odd.	We were awed by his words.

Does each word have the vowel [ɔ] or [a]. Circle [ɔ] or [a].

1. [ɔ] [a]   2. [ɔ] [a]   3. [ɔ] [a]   4. [ɔ] [a]   5. [ɔ] [a]

Repeat the phrases.

a strong lock   hot coffee   call a cop   watch the ball
a small doll   an odd wall   draw a clock   stop the song

B. Form sentences. Use *a lot of* or *all*. (*A lot of chalk is white.*)

 1. chalk/white   2. watch/have hands   3. hawk/eat meat
 4. cloth/soft   5. dog/have tails   6. lawn/easy to mow
 7. job/hard   8. bottle/made of glass   9. comic book/funny
10. ball/round   11. automobile/have tires 12. ponds/support wildlife

C. Form sentences. Tell someone to change clothes. Use *take off* and *put on*. (*Take off your good clothes and put on your old clothes.*)

 1. shoes/slippers   2. skirt/slacks   3. sweater/coat   4. clothes/bathrobe

D. Tell the placement of things in the picture. Use *on*. (*The plate is on the book. The book is on . . .*)

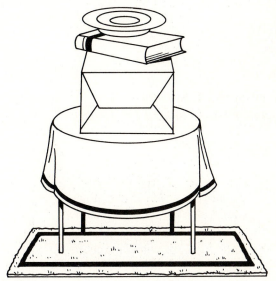

E. Tell what these people did on the camping trip. Use the past tense.

 1. Audrey/buy/fishing pole   2. Austin/bring/car   3. Bob/catch/fish
 4. Ronnie/shoot/hawk   5. Dawn/forget/golf ball 6. Paul/get/comic book
 7. Polly/lose/watch

LESSON 31

Not much luck:

The vowel [ə]

For [ə], your jaw and lips are relaxed and the middle of your tongue is raised slightly.

A. Listen and repeat.

uh	(Say the sound [ə], which is used by itself when hesitating.)		
	Well — uh — I'd like to — uh — think about that — uh — some more.		
tub	a big tub	a tub of water	a couple of tubs
cup	a small cup	a cup of tea	The cup's filled up.

Listen for the sound [ə]. Circle the corresponding number if you hear [ə] in the word.

1.   2.   3.   4.   5.   6.   7.   8.   9.   10.

Repeat the phrases.

11. enough gum   12. another bug   13. not much luck
    enough buses   another son   not much gum

B. Repeat the two forms of the verbs. Then repeat the phrases and use them in a sentence in the past tense. (*I hunted for Doug.*)

Present	Past	
hunt	hunted	hunt for Doug
love	loved	love our son
touch	touched	touch the stove
shut	shut	shut the window
cut	cut	cut my hand
win	won	win some money
dig	dug	dig a hole
sting	stung	sting my arm

C. Answer the questions below with full sentences. Use answers from this list.

Doug Somers	ducks	his thumb	the door of the truck
Miss Hubbard	a gold cup	for fun	the elephant's trunk

1. Who did Miss Hubbard love? (She loved Doug Somers.)
2. What did he hunt?

3. What did she touch?
4. What did he cut?
5. What did he shut?
6. Why did Doug dig a hole?
7. What did she win?
8. Who did the bee sting?

D. Tell what's the matter. Use *too* + an adjective + an infinitive. (*The baby's too young to run*.)

baby	meat	student	dull	rough	young	chew	drive on	study
knife	road	gloves	dumb	tough	old	cut	run	wear

E. Make up a short story using one of the phrases in Part B (*hunted for Doug*, etc.) and tell it to the class. Other students will listen and identify the phrase that was used.

(We were camping last week. My wife and I woke up early and were surprised that our young son, Doug, was not in the tent. We looked outside and he had disappeared! We called and looked everywhere, but did not see or hear him. We *hunted for Doug* for more than an hour. Finally we found him in the nearby woods trying to catch a squirrel.)

LESSON 32

Not much water:
Contrasting [ə] with [a], [æ], and [ɔ]

A. The sounds [ə] and [a]. Listen and repeat.

rub	Rob	Rob is cold.	He should rub his hands together.
done	Don	It was done for Don.	Now Don is done.
nut	not	This nut is not salty.	Those are not salty nuts.

Listen to two words. Do they both have the vowel [ə], do they both have [a], or do they have different vowels? Circle [ə], [a], or both [ə] and [a].

1. [ə] [a]   2. [ə] [a]
3. [ə] [a]   4. [ə] [a]
5. [ə] [a]   6. [ə] [a]

B. **Say the words in the table. Then say the given phrases and form some new ones.**

Modifiers	Verbs	Nouns	
some	cut	bus	luck
enough	touch	money	gum
a lot of	drop	box	clock
not much	watch	doll	water

Mod. + Noun

a lot of buses

enough water

_____

_____

Verb + Noun

touch the box

drop the money

_____

_____

C. **Tell the location of things in the picture. Use *on* and *under*. (*One duck is on the dock.*)**

D. **Listen and repeat. Then choose the correct answer, a or b.**

1. duck/dock

   Does the _____ need anything?

   a. Yes, a coat of paint.

   b. Yes, give it some rice.

2. rubber/robber

   Was that _____ really bad?

   a. Yes, he got away with $9,000.

   b. Yes, the tire wore out after 9,000 miles.

3. nuts/knots

Can you get rid of these _____ for me?

a. Sure, I'll eat them myself.

b. Sure, I'll untie them for you.

4. color/collar

Does the _____ of the shirt suit you?

a. No, it's too dark.

b. No, it's too large.

E. The sounds [ə] and [æ]. Listen and repeat.

rug	rag	Anne is saving rags.	She is making a rag rug.
cup	cap	Your cap is on the shelf.	Your cup is on the table.
uncle	ankle	My uncle hurt his ankle Monday.	"The ankle hurts," said my uncle.

F. Listen and repeat. Then choose the correct answer, a or b.

1. rug/rag

Is this _____ any good?

a. Yes, you can lay it on the floor.

b. Yes, you can clean the floor with it.

2. cup/cap

Can I borrow that _____ again?

a. Sure, but don't break the handle.

b. Sure, but don't get it wet.

3. uncle/ankle

What's the matter with your _____?

a. I hurt it.

b. He's got a cold.

4. truck/track

Why's the _____ so dirty?

a. It's been through a lot of mud.

b. People throw trash along it.

G. Form two sentences like the example. Use any subject pronoun. (*He rang the doorbell again. Now he's rung it four times.*)

ring the doorbell	begin to work	swim to the boat
sing that song	drink beer	run to school
shrink the shirt		

H. The sounds [ə] and [ɔ]. Listen and repeat.

cut	caught	She caught her finger in the door.	She cut it badly.
bus	boss	I saw my boss on the bus on Sunday.	My boss always rides the bus.
done	dawn	We'll be done at dawn.	It's dawn and we're done.

I. Form noun phrases. Use a modifier, adjective, and a singular or plural noun (*one young daughter*).

one	all	long	soft	ball	daughter	nut
some		small	young	bus	glove	song

LESSON 33

Good book:
The vowel [u]

For [**u**], your lips are rounded and the back of your tongue is raised.

A. Listen and repeat.

[u]	(Say the sound [u].)		
good	I feel good.	a good book	They look good today.
foot	I hurt my foot.	My foot hurts.	Look at my foot.

Listen for the sound [u]. Circle the corresponding number if you hear [u] in the word.

1.   2.   3.   4.   5.   6.   7.   8.   9.   10.

B. Repeat the verb forms. Then fill in the blanks with the past tense.

take/took   shake/shook   stand/stood   understand/understood

I went to the mayoral debate. The room was full. I _____ in the corner. Mr. Cushman _____ hands with his opponent. I _____ pictures of them. I _____ everything they said.

C. Tell someone to open or to move these things. Use *push* and *pull*. (*Please push the drawer shut*.)

drawer	elevator button
boots	electrical plug
car	front door

D. Tell someone where to put various things. (*Put the sock on your foot*.)

coat	icing	pudding	book	dish	hook
foot	marker	sock	cookie	foot	water

Form sentences. Tell things that you could do when you were six years old.

LESSON 34

Blue moon:
The vowel [uw]

For [**uw**], your lips are rounded and the back of your tongue is raised. Then the lips round more and the tongue moves slightly higher.

A. Listen and repeat.

[uw]	(Say the sound [uw].)		
food	some food	Have some food.	The food cooled.
suit	Get a suit	a new suit	a new blue suit

Listen for the sound [uw]. Circle the corresponding number if you hear [uw] in the word.

1.   2.   3.   4.   5.   6.   7.   8.   9.   10.

B. Form noun phrases. Use adjectives and nouns from the list.

blue	new		boot	room	moon
cool	two		pool	soup	suit

C. Form sentences. Use verbs and nouns from the list. (*Don't lose the shoe.*)

lose	shoot		goose	shoe
move	use		school	spoon

D. Your friend is helping you pick out a suit in a store. Use some or all of these words as you discuss your choice.

a few, through, who, you, too		dressing room, suit, shoe, truth
cool, blue, loose, smooth, new		choose, try on, fit, change, buy

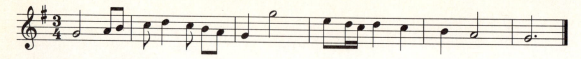

LESSON 35

Good food:
Contrasting [u] with [uw]

A. Listen and repeat.

pool	pull	Help her!	Pull her from the pool.
Luke	look	She'll look at Luke.	Will Luke look at her?
food	good	This food is good.	It's really good food.

Listen to pairs of words. Are they the same word or are their vowels different? Circle S or D.

1. S D   2. S D   3. S D
4. S D   5. S D   6. S D

Listen to each word. Circle the vowel sound which you hear.

7. [u] [uw]   8. [u] [uw]
9. [u] [uw]   10. [u] [uw]
11. [u] [uw]   12. [u] [uw]

B. A few words are pronounced with [uw] by some speakers and [u] by others. Listen to the voices on the tape pronounce them as the majority of people do. Circle the vowel that you hear.

1. Put this in the <u>room</u>.   [u] [uw]   2. Look at the horse's <u>hoof</u>.   [u] [uw]
3. He stood on the <u>roof</u>.   [u] [uw]   4. She pulled out the <u>root</u>.   [u] [uw]

C. Say the words in the table. Then say the given phrases and form some new ones.

Adjectives	Verbs (Past)		Nouns	
full	looked at	stood	book	woman
good	pulled	took	foot	wood
loose	pushed	cooked	boot	soup
blue	moved	drew	moon	suit
new	used	threw	shoe	spoon

Adj. + Noun	Verb + Noun
full moon _____	used my book _____
_____	_____

Now use some of the phrases in complete sentences. (*There's a full moon tonight.*)

Make questions with *who* + verb + noun. (*Who took my shoe?*)

D. Make *should I* questions. Use words from the table in Part C or any other words. Another student will give a short yes answer or no and a full sentence. (*Should I use my spoon? No. You should use your fork to eat beans with.*)

LESSON 36

Bob just bought two old books.
Summary of back vowels

A. Listen to each group of words. Then listen to them in a different order. Write numbers 1, 2, 3, and so on, to show the order that you hear them in.

1. look _____ Luke _____
   luck _____ lock _____

2. could _____ cooed _____
   cud _____ code _____
   cod _____ cawed _____

3. pull _____ pool _____
   Paul _____ pole _____

Form sentences. Use two of the words in each sentence. (*I will look for a new lock at the store.*)

B. Form a sentence from each group of words.

1.	books	two	2.	should	school	3.	good	blue
	just	old		from	home		one	Joe
	Bob	bought		Tom	walk		sock	lost

C. Listen, then fill in the blanks.

1. You _____ not _____ on the _____.
2. All of _____ good _____ are at the _____.
3. The _____ drawer is _____ of _____.

D. Play bingo. Choose one of these two cards. Listen to the words. Mark each word as you hear it. When a row (*vertical, horizontal, or diagonal*) is marked, you are a winner.

[uw]	[u]	[ə]	[ow]	[ɔ]
food	wood	fun	bone	walk
boot	look	bus	coat	cause
soon	full	FREE	hope	dawn
loose	put	blood	rose	bought
tube	bush	cut	home	off

[uw]	[u]	[ə]	[ow]	[ɔ]
loop	should	cup	most	boss
boot	wood	bus	bone	cause
food	look	FREE	coat	walk
soon	put	tub	rose	dawn
loose	full	blood	hope	bought

LESSON   37

The boy's toys:
The vowel [oy]

For [**oy**], your jaw begins open, lips are rounded, and the back of the tongue is slightly raised. Then the jaw closes somewhat, the lips spread, and the front of the tongue rises.

A. Listen and repeat.

[oy]	(Say the sound [oy].)		
toy	a new toy	a toy jeep	the boy's toys
coin	a new coin	coins and bills	Those are rare coins.
point	Don't point.	point a finger at	pointing at a coin

B. **Say these words. Then form a sentence telling something about them as they are in the picture.**

(He has a coin in his hand.)

boy

boy   point (verb)
coin   toy
joint

LESSON 38

Down and out:
The vowel [aw]

For [**aw**], your jaw begins open, lips are spread, and the front of the tongue is slightly raised. Then the jaw closes somewhat, the lips round, and the back of the tongue rises.

A. **Listen and repeat.**

ow	(Say the sound [aw], used as an expression of pain.)		
	Ow, this plate is hot!		
now	Do it now.	every now and then	Come out now.
loud	to talk loud	loud and clear	a loud sound
out	Let's get out.	out of town	down and out

B. **Discuss the weight of these things. Use** *how much, about, pounds, ounces, thousand.*

a cow	a flower	an owl (bird)	a hound (dog)
a towel	our house	a mouse	a pair of trousers (pants)

(How much does a cow weigh? About 1,200 pounds./More than a thousand pounds. Does a cow weigh 200 pounds? I doubt it. I think about 1,200 pounds.)

LESSON 39

A nice loud voice:

Contrasts involving [ay], [aw], [oy]

A. Listen to and repeat the contrasting words and the sentences. Form a sentence of your own for the last pair of words in each group.

1.	[ay]	my	[a]	Ma	"Dear Ma, please send my sweater."
		I'd		odd	I'd even do odd jobs for a living.
		like		lock	_____
2.	[oy]	soy	[ɔ]	saw	I saw the soy sauce on the table.
		Joyce		caught	Joyce caught a cold.
		oil		all	_____
3.	[ay]	buy	[oy]	boy	Each boy will buy one notebook.
		lied		Lloyd	Do you think Lloyd lied about it?
		pint		point	_____
4.	[ay]	high	[aw]	how	How high is Coit Tower?
		find		found	She found him before he could find her.
		mice		mouse	_____

B. Listen to these five words beginning with [r]: row, rye, Roy, rah, raw. Now listen to three sentences. For each sentence write the numbers 1, 2, 3, and so on, beside the words that you hear in the order that you hear them. (*All five of the words may not be in each sentence.*)

1. row ____	rye ____	Roy ____	rah ____	raw ____
2. row ____	rye ____	Roy ____	rah ____	raw ____
3. row ____	rye ____	Roy ____	rah ____	raw ____

C. Form sentences with two words from each of these groups.

1. rouse/rise/Roy's   2. pies/poise/pa's/paws   3. rout/right/rot/wrought

D. Repeat the phrases. Use them in completing the sentences.

a frightening noise   a pound of rice   join a bicycle club
a nice, loud voice   a thousand eyes   point out the mistake

1. The child cried when _____.   2. Night has _____.

3. The recipe calls for _____.   4. If you want to get exercise, _____.

5. The teacher will help by _____.   6. When you speak to the class, _____.

LESSON   40

Is your car here or there?

Vowels before [r]

A. Listen and repeat.

are [ar]	ear [ir]	air [er]	or [ɔr]	[ur]
car	here	there	door	your

Where's your car?   Is your car here?   No, our car's there.
We're here.   You're there.   They're here, too.

B. Repeat the noun phrases. Then form new ones using words in the table.

Modifiers	Adjectives		Nouns	
our	dark	short	arm	door
your	large	sore	car	fork
their	sharp	warm	yard	hair

Mod. + Noun   Adj. + Noun

their arms   dark hair

_____   _____

C. Read the paragraphs and then finish the story. Use words from this lesson or from the list below.

A driver was speeding down the road. He was sure someone was following him. The driver was Charles Barry, a reporter for a newspaper. He had a story, an important one. Someone from a foreign embassy had just given him some secret papers.

Charles looked in the rearview mirror. Suddenly a curve loomed ahead. He jerked the wheel. His car swerved, and . . .

Nouns: cornfield, deer, fire, floor, guard, heart, marsh, morning, storm, torch
Verbs: carry, fear, form, hear, park, pour, roar, scare, tear, warn
Adjectives: far, fierce, narrow, near, poor, rare, sure, torn, worn

D. **Contrasts involving vowels before [r]. Listen and repeat.**

are	ah	or	awe	ear	E	air	A	tour	too
heart	hot	sore	saw	near	knee	there	they	sure	shoe
sharp	shop	court	caught	beard	bead	stairs	stays		

E. **Repeat the sentences.**

Here's Mark.   I want to draw.   Your hair is terrible.
He is here.   There's paper in the drawer.   It looks like hay.

Now form sentences. Use pairs of words from Part D. (I see Jay and Claire. *There* they *are.*)

F. **A barber (or hairdresser) and customer are talking. The customer tells how he wants his hair done (perhaps he has brought a picture of what he wants). The barber offers suggestions. Use any words from this lesson or from the following lists.**

hair, beard, curl, sideburns, part,   comb, brush, blow-dry, style,
perm, short, sharp, chair, here, there   shampoo, long, tease, roller

LESSON   41

A hurt bird:
The vowel [ᵊr]

For [ᵊ**r**] the front of your tongue is raised and curled back slightly. The lower lip may stick out a little.

A. **Listen and repeat.**

[ᵊr]   (Say the sound [ᵊr].)

her   I know her.   her glasses   Her name is Shirley.

heard   We heard.   I heard Joan.   I heard a bird.

hurt   She's hurt.   It hurt Joan.   I see a hurt bird.

Listen for the sound [ᵊr]. Circle the corresponding number if you hear [ᵊr] in the word.

1.   2.   3.   4.   5.   6.   7.   8.   9.   10.

B. **Repeat the adjectives and nouns. Then form noun phrases with them.**

| dirty | third | bird | nurse |
| nervous | thirsty | clerk | shirt |

C. **Form sentences like the examples.** (*The girls were thirsty. Herb learned the word.*)

1. girls/thirsty   2. clerks/nervous   3. shirts/dirty   4. skirts/worse
5. learned/word   6. burned/curtain   7. heard/bird   8. hurt/girl

D. **The sounds [ᵊr] and [ə] and [a]. Listen and repeat.**

bird	bud	Bud got a bird.	her	ha	Ha, I know her.
burn	bun	Don't burn the bun.	term	Tom	Tom is away this term.
Kurt	cut	Kurt cut himself.	clerk	clock	The clerk watches the clock.

Listen to pairs of words. Are they the same word or are their vowels different? Circle S or D.

1. S   D   2. S   D   3. S   D
4. S   D   5. S   D   6. S   D

Listen to each word. Circle the vowel sound which you hear.

7. [ᵊr]   [ə]   8. [ᵊr]   [a]
9. [ᵊr]   [ə]   10. [ᵊr]   [a]
11. [ᵊr]   [ə]   12. [ᵊr]   [a]

E. **Form sentences. Use both words in each sentence.**

1. hurt/hot   2. shirt/shut   3. dirt/dot   4. search/such
5. earn/on   6. Herb/tub   7. burned/bond   8. third/thud

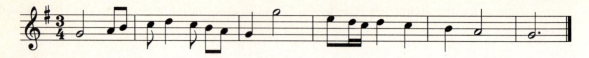

LESSON 42

Cora is in the chorus.

The unstressed vowel [ə]

A. Repeat the words and then the sentences.

1. I'm getting a visa for Burma.
   I need a visa to go to Burma.
2. China is on the east coast of Asia.
   Everyone knows that China is in Asia.
3. Zebras and pandas are black and white.
   The zebra's in Kenya and the panda's in China.

Now form sentences that describe the differences between China and Burma and zebras and pandas.

B. Repeat these sentences. Remember your tongue is curled back for [ər].

1. Dinah isn't the owner of the diner. Dinah's daughter owns the diner.
2. Stella gave a stellar performance. The words stellar and Stella both refer to "star."
3. He's a piano tuner. He brought a tuna sandwich with him for lunch today.

C. Circle the syllable or syllables that have the weak vowel [ə].

1.	phar·(ma)·cist	2.	pres·i·dent
3.	com·plete·ly	4.	el·e·phant
5.	A·las·ka	6.	mu·si·cian
7.	tel·e·phone	8.	al·pha·bet
9.	pho·to·graph	10.	to·bac·co
11.	ba·na·na	12.	gas·o·line
13.	en·e·my	14.	cor·rect·ly

D. Repeat these words. Then listen to the sentences and fill in the words.

around   about   balloon   machine   Cora   Flora   chorus   florist

1. Don't play _____ the _____.   2. _____ works for a _____.

3. I know a story _____ a _____.   4. _____ is in the _____.

E. Listen to this reading. Pay particular attention to the underlined syllables with the [ə] sound. Then read it aloud.

Adele Marcus went to the supermarket today. She was having a party and had a lot of things to buy. She was also in a great hurry.

She went up one aisle and down another. She bought bananas, lettuce, potatoes, and carrots. She bought meat and rolls. Then it happened! Somebody took her basket.

She looked and looked—and looked some more. Finally, she found it. A small child was pushing it. An elderly man with the boy apologized. "It was a mistake," he said.

What do you think Adele said?

LESSON 43

Older, wiser, and richer:

The unstressed vowel [ər]

A. Listen to and repeat each *-er* word. Then repeat the phrases.

other sugar	either razor	never offer
under water	either ladder	silver dollar

Use two or three of the phrases in full sentences. (*There's sand or something in this sugar. Where's the other sugar?*)

B. The suffix *-er* forms the comparative form of the adjective. It shows that there is more of that adjective. Listen and repeat.

hotter	bigger	older	wiser	slower
warmer	longer	nearer	taller	finer
deeper	richer	nicer	safer	higher

Form noun phrases with the above comparative adjectives (*a hotter day, etc.*) Then use the noun phrases in a complete sentence. (*This is a hotter day.*)

C. The *-er* suffix can also be added to many verbs to form a noun that indicates which person or thing does the action of the verb. Many are names of occupations. Listen and repeat.

baker	trader	robber	scorer	racer
singer	winner	dreamer	swimmer	loser
waiter	shopper	teacher	diver	washer

D. Form sentences using the above nouns and these names: Peter, Grover, Mr. Carter, Miss Tucker, Kroner, Miller. (*Peter is an Olympic diver.*)

E. The object pronoun *her* is often unstressed. In colloquial speech it is pronounced *'er* and is spoken as if attached to the preceding word. Listen and repeat each phrase and sentence, then form a new sentence with the same phrase.

Preposition + *her*

1. There was no mail for'er. (I did an errand for'er.)
2. I got a letter from'er.
3. We gave a present to'er.
4. He threw a book at'er.
5. It was thoughtful of'er.
6. Jim sat down beside'er.
7. There was a noise behind'er.
8. He went to a movie without'er.

F. Repeat the phrases. Stress the verb and use weak stress with the object pronoun *'er*.

Verb + *her*

take'er	need'er	pay'er	blame'er	call'er
bring'er	phone'er	tell'er	teach'er	love'er
get'er	stop'er	rob'er	kiss'er	show'er

Read the sentence and fill in the proper verbs followed by 'er.

1. I'll ___take'er___ home. Someone might _____ and _____. (rob, take, stop)

2. He _____ because he _____. (loved, kissed)

3. I can't _____ now. I'll _____ later. I want to _____ something. (tell, phone, call)

4. They didn't _____ for the gas. She's upset. I don't _____. (blame, pay)

5. We _____ on the team. Will someone _____ and _____ here? (bring, need, get)

G. The possessive modifier *her* is just like the object pronoun. Listen and repeat the sentences.

Auxiliary + *her* + subject

Is her husband home?

Does her dress look good?

Was her bus late?

Do her children talk yet?

<u>Can't her</u> husband help?
It <u>must be her</u> mother.
<u>Won't her</u> car start?
<u>Couldn't her</u> brother come?

Other function (grammar) words + *her*

She lost <u>all her</u> jewelry.
She's French, <u>but her</u> husband's Dutch.
Sue caught cold. <u>Then her</u> husband did.
She had a cold. <u>Now her</u> husband does.

Now complete the sentences by using one of the auxiliaries or function words from the list followed by *her.*

1. She spent __half__ __her__ money on it.
2. _____ _____ children go to school?
3. _____ _____ parents coming to visit?
4. Nancy _____ _____ friend went shopping.
5. _____ _____ dishwasher broken?
6. Julie speaks French, _____ _____ friend doesn't.

| do | half | are |
| is | but | and |

H. Tell about your relatives. Use comparative adjectives and mention their occupations or other things that they do. (*My sister is younger than I am. She loves airplanes and wants to be a flier.*)

LESSON 44

Children giggle:
The unstressed syllables [ᵊl] and [ᵊn]

A. Listen and repeat each [ᵊl] noun.

pickle	table	novel	castle	tunnel
bottle	apple	puzzle	camel	barrel

Form noun phrases using the words with *little* or *middle* and use them in sentences. (I bought a jar of *little pickles*. I can't reach the salt *in the middle of the table*.)

B. Many *-le* verbs refer to a repetitive sound or movement. Repeat the *-le* words; then form sentences. (*The children giggled. Ben bobbled the ball.*)

children	crackle	ball	bobble
coins	giggle	loose handle	twiddle
fire	jingle	star	twinkle
leaves	rattle	thumbs	wiggle
windows	rustle	worm	wobble

C. The auxiliary *will* is often unstressed. It is pronounced [ᵊl] and spoken as if attached to the preceding word. Listen to and repeat each phrase and sentence. Then form a new sentence with the same phrase. (*Jack'll need his heavy sweater for the trip.*)

1. Jack'll study Spanish next year.
2. The park'll be closed for a month.
3. Bob'll take Mary to the dance.
4. Her raise'll begin on July first.
5. Tom'll be back from vacation soon.
6. Your watch'll need cleaning.
7. Ann'll be surprised to hear it.
8. The meeting'll be at nine.
9. Claire'll answer the phone.
10. The store'll be open until six.

D. Listen and repeat each [ᵊn] word.

wagon	sudden	open	kitchen	legion	raisin	common	melon
chicken	cotton	region	seven	muffin	lesson	cannon	foreign

Form three phrases or sentences. Use at least two of the words in each. (*The young man ran away and joined the French foreign legion.*)

The suffix *-en* is added to some words (mostly adjectives) and forms a verb. For example, *short–shorten*, meaning "to become shorter" or "to make (something) shorter."

E. Add *-en* to the words below and pronounce the resulting verbs.

   deep/wide   length/short   ripe/sweet   loose/straight

F. Make sentences using these given names and family names. (*The new student's name is Helen Reardon.*)

Ethan	Karen	Bacon	Mason	Shippen
Gretchen	Megan	Griffin	Patton	
Helen	Robin	Hazen	Reardon	

LESSON   45

Very yellow:

The unstressed vowels [iʸ] and [oʷ]

These weak vowels are shorter in length than their stressed forms [**iy**] and [**ow**].

A. Listen and repeat each -y word. Then repeat the phrases.

every baby	any money	very happy	these babies
every city	any jelly	very sorry	these cities

Now use the phrases in sentences. (*Every baby has a bottle.*)

B. Many words ending with [iʸ] (spelled *-y* or *-ie*) are words of endearment. Listen to these names and match them with the forms printed below. Write numbers 1 through 10.

___ Arch	___ Dad	___ Jim	_1_ Ron	___ Tom
___ Bob	___ George	___ John	___ Steve	___ Will

C. The suffix *-y* is added to many nouns to form an adjective. Listen to and repeat the noun base and the adjective. (sun–sunny)

sunny	cloudy	stormy
rainy	windy	snowy

foggy	chilly	icy
muddy	dusty	starry

Describe the weather where you are. Use the modifiers *very* and *pretty*.

D. Repeat these adjectives, verbs, and nouns that end with weak [oʷ]. Then form sentences using at least two of the words. (*The crowd followed the hero of the game.*)

narrow	borrow	fellow	pillow	window
yellow	follow	hero	shadow	zero

E. Some shortened words end with [oʷ]. Listen to these shortened words and match them with the full forms below. Write numbers 1 through 6.

____ automobile   ____ hippopotamus   ____ memorandum
____ photograph   ____ rhinoceros   ____ typographical error

F. Repeat the phrases. Then use some of them in answering the questions.

a happy fellow	very yellow	borrow some money
a narrow valley	pretty heavy	carry the hero

1. What is she looking at? (She's looking at a very yellow dress.)
2. Where do they live?
3. What did they do after the game?
4. How are they going to pay the bill?
5. What kind of person is he?

 UNIT FOUR

Grammar Words and Intonation

The relatively small number of grammar words (articles, pronouns, auxiliary verbs, prepositions, etc.) occur very often, and they relate to the other parts of speech (nouns, verbs, adjectives, adverbs) in the sentence. Many grammar words are weakly stressed or contracted and joined to another word. In this section you will practice some contractions of the auxiliary verb *be* and pronunciation of the articles. You will begin with the intonation of counting, words in a series, and alternative questions.

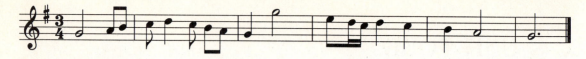

LESSON 46

One, two, buckle your shoe.
Counting intonation

A. You will hear people count with three different intonations. Listen and repeat.

1. Slow counting with falling intonation on each number.

   one   two   three   four   five   six   seven   eight   nine   ten

2. Sometimes counting has rising intonation on all numbers except the last, which has falling intonation. In counting, the "teen" numbers are stressed on the first syllable.

   eleven   twelve   thirteen   fourteen   fifteen   sixteen   seventeen

   eighteen   nineteen   twenty

3. Faster counting may have level intonation. All numbers are spoken with level intonation, except the last number which has falling intonation.

   ten   twenty   thirty   forty   fifty   sixty   seventy   eighty   ninety   one hundred

   Count by twos to twenty using rising intonation. (two, four . . .)

   Count by threes to twenty-one using level intonation. (three, six . . .)

   Count by fives to fifty slowly, using falling intonation on each number. (five, ten . . .)

B. Listen to the numbers. They are read in groups of various lengths. Mark the falling intonation at the end of each group with the arrow (⌒).

1. 1   2   3   4   5   6   7   8   9   10   11   12   13   14   15   16   17   18   19   20
2. 10   11   12   13   14   15   16   17   18   19   20   21   22   23   24   25   26   27   28
3. 51   52   53   54   55   56   57   58   59   60   61   62   63   64   65   66   67   68   69

Now listen to the letters of the alphabet. They are read in groups of various lengths. Mark the falling intonation at the end of each group with the arrow (⌒).

4. A B C D E F G H I J K L M N O P Q R S T U V W X Y Z
5. A B C D E F G H I J K L M N O P Q R S T U V W X Y Z
6. A B C D E F G H I J K L M N O P Q R S T U V W X Y Z

C. Listen to these words being spelled. Mark a falling arrow (⌐) at the end of each word.

R O S E S A R E R E D V I O L E T S A R E B L U E

S U G A R I S S W E E T A N D S O A R E Y O U

D. Listen to this children's counting rhyme. Mark the falling intonations you hear with the arrow (⌐).

One, two, buckle your shoe.
Three, four, open the door.
Five, six, pick up sticks.
Seven, eight, shut the gate.
Nine, ten, do it again.

E. In English, words are read in groups. This helps make the meaning clear. In reading mathematical expressions, numbers in parentheses are read as a group. Listen.

1. $(2 \times 4) + 3 = 11$ (Two times four) plus three equals eleven.
2. $2 \times (4 + 3) = 14$ Two times (four plus three) is   fourteen.
3. $(3 \times 5) + 10$
4. $3 \times (5 + 10)$
5. $9 - (2 + 6)$
6. $(9 - 2) + 6$

F. Listen, and add the parentheses correctly.

1. $(7 + 2) + 4$ 2. $10 \times 3 + 7$ 3. $8 + 2 \times 2$ 4. $1 + 9 \times 3$
5. $7 \times 2 + 4$ 6. $6 \times 5 + 2$ 7. $3 - 5 \times 5$ 8. $15 - 5 \times 3$

G. Write the equations you hear. Then circle the correct answer.

1. _____ = 70   25   2. _____ = 150   50
3. _____ = 35   350   4. _____ = 120   56

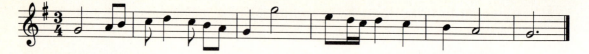

LESSON 47

Apples, bananas, and oranges:
Intonation of words in series

A. Listen and repeat. The numbers are said with rising intonation but have falling intonation at the end of each group.

1 2 3 4   5 6 7 8 9 10 11 12 13 14 15 16 17 18 19 20

Now listen, and mark the falling intonation at the end of each group of numbers and letters.

1 2 3 4 5 6 7 8 9 10 11 12 13 14 15 16 17 18 19 20
A B C D E F G H I J K L M N O P Q R S T U V W X Y Z

B. Listen and repeat. The same kind of rising intonation is used with words in series.

apples, bananas, and oranges   speak, read, and write   Harriet, Robert, and Will

Complete the sentences 1 through 6 with a series of words a through f.

(*For breakfast I have cereal, coffee, and juice.*)

1. For breakfast I have . . .		a. talent	experience	ambition
2. Bill speaks . . .		b. cereal	coffee	juice
3. That little boy is . . .		c. hungry	sleepy	tired
4. Mr. Novak is buying some . . .		d. basketball	soccer	baseball
5. Ms. Gomez has a lot of . . .		e. shirts	ties	socks
6. Sally is a good athlete. She plays . . .		f. English	French	Spanish

C. Now pretend you are a waiter in a restaurant. Describe the foods that are available to the diners.

Our entrees this evening are _____, _____, and _____.

For vegetables we have _____, _____, and _____.

Suggestions: *soups* (tomato, pea, onion); *vegetables* (peas, carrots, tomatoes); *salad dressings* (French, Russian, oil and vinegar); *entrees* (roast chicken, fried shrimp, spaghetti); *potatoes* (whipped, baked, French fries); *desserts* (fruit, ice cream, cake); *beverages* (coffee, tea, milk).

LESSON   48

Coffee, tea, or milk?
Intonation of alternative questions

When a person is asked to make a choice between two things, a high-rising intonation (as in a yes-no question) is used with the first choice in the question and a falling intonation on the second. A vertical line indicates that the sentence is said in two phrases.

A. Listen to and repeat the questions.

Do you want | coffee⌐ | or \t⌐e↓a   Was it | Sally⌐ | or Hel⌐en

We indicate this intonation by using a rising arrow (⌐) and a falling arrow (⌐).

Is it John | or Fred?   Is Billy hungry | or tired?
Was your sister happy | or sad?

B. Now form questions. Ask someone to make a choice between two things. Begin with one of the phrases below and select two of the three appropriate items in the list. (Do you like baseball or soccer?)

1.	Do you like . . . ?	coffee	tea	milk
2.	Who called? Was it . . . ?	John	Roberto	Paul
3.	Are you studying . . . ?	New York	London	Paris
4.	Would you like . . . ?	the post office	the shoe store	the bank
5.	Was that woman . . . ?	basketball	baseball	soccer
6.	Does your son play . . . ?	her mother	her sister	a friend
7.	Are you going to . . . ?	Chinese	Japanese	Vietnamese
8.	Is Gloria going to marry . . . ?	walk	drive	take the bus

C. Listen carefully. Then repeat the phrases. In these questions there are three choices.

coffee, tea, or milk   Hondas, Volvos, or Toyotas   math, science, or history

Repeat the sentences.

Would you like coffee, tea, or milk?

Do they sell Hondas, Volvos, or Toyotas?

Are you studying math, science, or history?

D. Ask questions that require the listener to make a choice among two or three things. As suggestions, ask about:

(1) the kind of car someone drives (*Does Jim drive a Ford or a Chevrolet?*)
(2) someone's nationality, birthplace, or native language (*Is your native language Chinese, Korean, or Japanese?*)
(3) favorite kind of entertainment (*Do you prefer to go to the movies, read, or watch television?*)
(4) favorite vacation spots or cities (*Would you like to see London, New York, or Rio de Janeiro?*)
(5) favorite mode of transporation (*Do you prefer traveling by train, plane, or car?*)
(6) favorite kinds of foods, as on a menu (*Would you like peas, carrots, or potatoes?*)

LESSON   49

He's coming?

When statements get question intonation

A. A statement may become a question by the use of rising intonation. Listen to the following statements and questions.

Statement	*Question*
He's coming.	He's coming?
She knows him.	She knows him?
They didn't want to come.	They didn't want to come?

Often the use of the rising intonation with a statement-order question indicates surprise or incredulity. Listen.

He's forty-two.   He's forty-two?   (I can't believe it! He doesn't look that old.)

That's his wife.   That's his wife?   (I can't believe that woman is his wife. I'm very surprised.)

B. **Listen. If the sentences are read with a rising intonation, use a question mark (?). If read with a falling intonation (a statement), use a period (.).**

Punctuation

1. That's your sister
2. You didn't see her
3. He didn't answer
4. We weren't invited
5. She was born in China
6. They speak Portuguese
7. He's a psychologist
8. You know her

C. **Listen to these exchanges. Explain the rising intonation.**

1.
   a. My sister's coming tomorrow.
   b. Your sister?
      I didn't know you had a sister.

2.
   a. I failed the math exam.
   b. You failed it?
      I don't believe it. You're so good in math.

3.
   a. I want you to meet my mother.
   b. Your mother? I can't believe it. She looks like your sister.

4.
   a. I knew your father.
   b. You knew my father?
   a. Yes. He and my father were friends.

LESSON 50

Where? When?

Question-word questions — with rising and falling intonation

A. **Question-word questions normally ask for information and have falling intonation.**

What's her name? Marie.   Where does she live? In Paris.

Sometimes the listener does not hear or understand and asks the speaker to repeat. He or she may do this by asking "What did you say?" or simply, "What?"

Our son's a doctor.

What did you say?

I said our son's a doctor.

I'm going swimming.

What?

I said I'm going swimming.

B. **If a speaker doesn't understand a reply to a question-word question, he or she may ask the listener to repeat. To do this, the speaker may simply repeat the question word with rising intonation, or repeat the entire question. Listen.**

Where does your daughter live?	Who's your teacher?	When are you leaving?
She's living in Montreal.	Mr. Farmer.	Next week.
Where does she live?	Who?	When?
In Montreal.	Mr. Farmer.	Next week.

Listen to the intonation of the question words in the following exchanges.

Asking for Information   Asking for Repetition

1. Marie lives in France now.   2. Marie lives in France now.
       Where?   Where?
   In Paris.   In France.

3. A friend of mine won a trip to New   4. Harriet Summeril won the annual art
   York.   contest.
       Who?   Harriet who?
   Jim White.   Summeril. Harriet Summeril.

C. **First read these conversations. Then take the part of Speaker B.**

1.
   A. My car was stolen.
   B. When?
   A. Just a few minutes ago.
   B. When?
   A. Just a few minutes ago.

2.
   A. I was in Chicago last week.
   B. When?
   A. Last week.
   B. When?
   A. On Tuesday and Wednesday.

3.
   A. When are you leaving for Japan?
   B. Next month.
   A. When?
   B. On the fourteenth.
   A. When?
   B. On the fourteenth.

4.
   A. Where did you see him last?
   B. In Georgia.
   A. Where?
   B. I said in Georgia.
   A. Where?
   B. In Atlanta.

D. **Listen to these exchanges. Pay particular attention to the intonation of the question word. Then circle the correct response, a or b.**

1. There was a big explosion in Texas.
       Where?
   a. In Texas.   b. In Houston.

2. Someone broke something in my office yesterday.
       What?
   a. Someone broke something in my office.   b. My desk lamp.

3. I'll meet you later this afternoon.
   When?
   a. Later this afternoon.   b. At four o'clock.

4. Guess what I just found!
   What?
   a. I said guess what I found.   b. A twenty-dollar bill.

LESSON   51

Helen was eighteen.

Stress of numbers

A. **Listen and repeat. Numbers such as twenty-one, thirty-six, and forty-nine have the stress on the last word.**

• ´	• ´	• ´
twenty-one	forty-seven	sixty-four
twenty-two	forty-eight	sixty-five
twenty-three	forty-nine	sixty-six
thirty-four	fifty-one	seventy-seven
thirty-five	fifty-two	eighty-eight
thirty-six	fifty-three	ninety-nine

B. **Listen to the number. Then say the next number with falling intonation and write it down.**

(41) __42__ _____ _____ _____ _____ _____

C. **Listen to the number. Then say the next number in reverse.**

(67) __76__ _____ _____ _____ _____ _____

D. **Now listen to and repeat these pairs of numbers. The stress of *-teen* numbers contrasts with that of the *-ty* numbers.**

´	´	´	´
thirteen	thirty	seventeen	seventy
fourteen	forty	eighteen	eighty
fifteen	fifty	nineteen	ninety
sixteen	sixty		

Circle the number you hear.

1. 18 80   2. 14 40   3. 17 70   4. 13 30   5. 15 50
6. 19 90   7. 15 50   8. 16 60   9. 14 40   10. 13 30

E. Write the number you hear.

1. Uncle John is __70__ years old.

2. Our house is _____ years old.

3. There are _____ teachers in our school.

4. Did you say Helen was _____ or _____ years old?

5. There are _____ boys in this class.

6. I need _____ dollars.

7. This pen costs _____ cents.
   That one costs _____ cents.

F. Tell the people's ages. Use full sentences.

1. The king was born in 1210.   How old was he in 1260? (He was fifty.)
2. Tom was born in 1970.   How old is he this year?
3. Mrs. Chung was born in 1949.   How old was she in 1979?
4. Robert Todd was born in 1608.   How old was he in 1658?
5. The twins were born in 1983.   How old will they be in 1999?

LESSON   52

Eight dollars and sixty-five cents:
Stress of numbers as modifiers

Numbers usually have strong stress when used before a noun.

A. Listen and repeat.

two   two books   sixty-seven   sixty-seven cents
eight   eight women   thirty   thirty classrooms
nineteen   nineteen dollars   thirteen   thirteen cities

B. Repeat the prices. Often when giving prices, two phrases are used.

$4.29   four dollars | and twenty-nine cents

$42.40   forty-two dollars | and forty cents

Tell how much these articles cost. (The cassettes cost $8.65.)

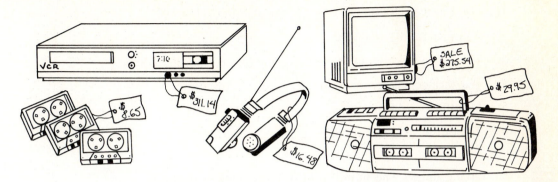

C. Make sentences from these sentence subjects, verbs, and objects. Use any logical number. (*Our school has thirty-two teachers.*)

SUBJECTS: school, building, Mr. Pappas, everyone, the Norse Bus Line, Mrs. Ryan
VERBS: has, costs, owns, bought, operates
OBJECTS: classrooms, teachers, buses, fingers, suits, sweaters, offices, students

D. Form sentences using numbers about things around you, for example, pages in a book, students in class, floors in a building, buses in the city, cars in the parking lot, games your team won, and so on. Use *about* if you don't know the exact numbers. (*This book has ninety-six pages./There are about ninety-six pages in this book.*)

LESSON 53

June third, 1985:
Giving dates and addresses

A. Ordinal numbers. Listen and repeat. Except for first, second, third, twenty-first, and so on, all ordinal numbers end in the sound [th].

1st	first	20th	twentieth	59th	fifty-ninth
2nd	second	21st	twenty-first	44th	forty-fourth
3rd	third	26th	twenty-sixth	95th	ninety-fifth
4th	fourth	37th	thirty-seventh	84th	eighty-fourth
5th	fifth	48th	forty-eighth	66th	sixty-sixth

B. **Fill in the blanks with any reasonable ordinal number.**

1. Jason is the __fourth__ child in the family.

2. Apartment 1701 is on the _____ floor.

3. The Sanchezes live in the _____ house from the corner.

4. Our theater tickets are in the _____ row center.

5. My office is on the _____ floor.

6. Tomorrow will be Howard's _____ birthday.

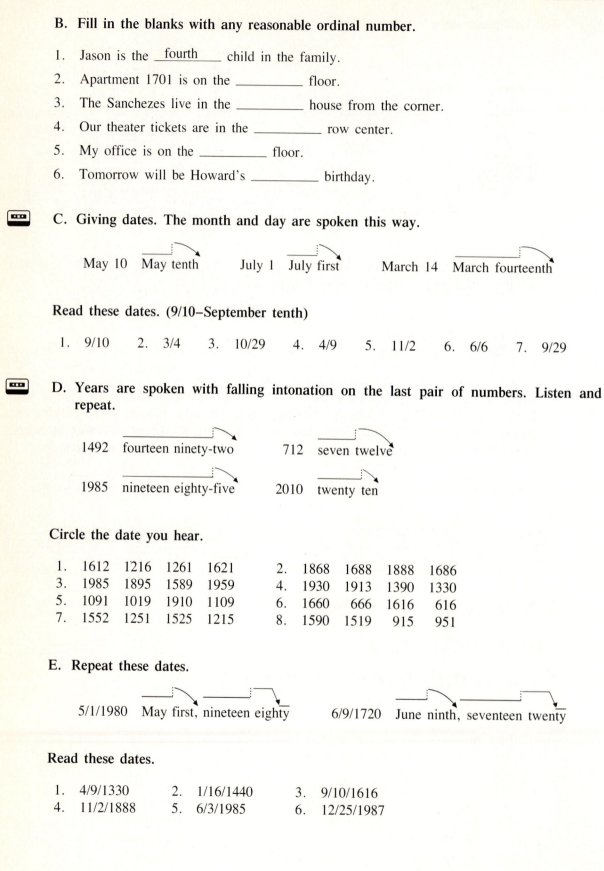

C. **Giving dates. The month and day are spoken this way.**

May 10   May tenth   July 1   July first   March 14   March fourteenth

Read these dates. (9/10–September tenth)

1. 9/10   2. 3/4   3. 10/29   4. 4/9   5. 11/2   6. 6/6   7. 9/29

D. **Years are spoken with falling intonation on the last pair of numbers. Listen and repeat.**

1492   fourteen ninety-two   712   seven twelve

1985   nineteen eighty-five   2010   twenty ten

Circle the date you hear.

1. 1612   1216   1261   1621   2. 1868   1688   1888   1686
3. 1985   1895   1589   1959   4. 1930   1913   1390   1330
5. 1091   1019   1910   1109   6. 1660   666   1616   616
7. 1552   1251   1525   1215   8. 1590   1519   915   951

E. **Repeat these dates.**

5/1/1980   May first, nineteen eighty   6/9/1720   June ninth, seventeen twenty

Read these dates.

1. 4/9/1330   2. 1/16/1440   3. 9/10/1616
4. 11/2/1888   5. 6/3/1985   6. 12/25/1987

F. Giving addresses. Listen.

1621 Elm Street	sixteen twenty-one Elm Street
2962 14th Street	twenty-nine sixty-two Fourteenth Street
712 21st Street	seven twelve Twenty-first Street

Zip codes are read as a sequence of five numbers: 54516 — five four five one six.

G. These people applied for passports recently. Ask about their addresses, birth dates, ages, and destinations. (*What's Mr. Macias's address? 1490 Clayton Street. What is his zip code? When was Foster Colby born? Where is he planning to go?*)

Name	Address	Zip Code	Date of Birth	Destination
John D. Macias	1490 Clayton Street Denver, Colorado	80218	3/1/15	Tokyo
Susan B. Antonelli	1919 Morrison Street Dallas, Texas	75208	9/16/63	Moscow
Pat Rae Sheeler	830 Second Street Mason City, Iowa	50401	1/10/55	London
Mary Ellen Fox	2732 South Street Madison, Wisconsin	53715	12/24/52	Buenos Aires
Foster R. Colby	7213 Spring Street Tampa, Florida	33614	6/26/39	Bangkok
Robert G. Quon	614 Main Street Cheyenne, Wyoming	82001	5/7/46	Stockholm

LESSON 54

Cups and saucers:
Pronunciation of plural nouns

A. Read each noun and pronounce the plural form.

eye	neck	cheek
eyelash	arm	lip
nose	hand	leg
ear	finger	toe

Plural Endings of Nouns		
After a noun that ends with the sound	*The plural ending is*	*Examples*
[p] [t] [k] [f] [th]	[s]	lips cakes
[s] [z] [sh] [sh] [ch] [j]	[ᵊz]	noses dishes
all other sounds	[z]	eyes, beds arms

B. Ask the prices of these articles. (*How much are the plates? They're eight dollars.*)

plate ($8.00)	fork ($3.00)
cup ($6.00)	spoon ($3.00)
saucer ($6.00)	napkin ($4.00)
glass ($5.00)	soup bowl ($7.00)

Ask how many of certain articles you can buy for a certain amount of money.

How many spoons can you buy (get) for one hundred dollars? You can get thirty-three spoons.

C. Read each noun and pronounce the plural form.

1. lamp	2. toy	3. chair	4. skirt	5. belt
6. baseball	7. watch	8. glove	9. book	10. purse
11. blouse	12. robe	13. bed	14. dish	15. broom
16. ring	17. birdcage	18. clock	19. sofa	20. rug

You are in a large department store. Ask a salesperson for information. Use one of the question models below. Use appropriate nouns from the list.

1	• Misses Fashion Accessories • Jewelry • Sportswear • Men's Clothing Furnishings and Sportswear • Toiletries • Hats • Stationery • Greeting Cards • Notions • Gift Shop • Luggage • Gift Certificates
2	• Intimate Apparel • Shoe Salon • Boys Wear • Children's World • Young Juniors • Maternity Wear
3	• Misses and Women's Better Apparel • Furs • Bridal Shop • Wigs • Misses and Petites Better Sportswear
4	• Table Linens • Bedspreads • Blankets • Sheets • Bed Pillows • Curtains • Throw Pillows • Bath Shop • China • Art Porcelain • Glassware • Candles • Waterford • Silver • Gift Shop • Wedding Gift Registry
5	• Books • Lamps • Housewares and Electric Appliances • Rugs • Carpeting • Home Decorating • Fabrics • Portrait Studio • American Express Travel • Ladies' Rest Room
6	• Misses and Women's Dresses • Coats • Casual Dresses • Suits • Sportswear • Shoes • Beauty Shop • Furniture Service • Adjustments • Business Offices • Cashiers • Lost and Found • Men's Rest Room
7	• Traditional and Contemporary Furniture • Mattresses • Sofa Beds • Recliners • Model Rooms • Interior Decorators
8	• Rare Books • Television • Stereo • Records • Cameras • Art Gallery • Toys • Art Needlework • Summer Furniture • Employment • Ladies' Rest Room • Men's Rest Room

Where are the lamps?/I'm looking for the lamps./Excuse me, can you tell me where the lamps are?
Yes. They're in the furniture department. That's on the fifth floor.

D. **Form questions like the models. Try to form questions about things that are around you in your school, home, city, or country. (*How many days does a week have? How many wings does a bird have?*)**

1. day/week
2. wing/bird
3. park/this city
4. university/your country
5. library/this city
6. door/car
7. lamp/your bedroom
8. page/book
9. chair/your office
10. teacher/school
11. book/the library

E. **Listen to the questions and requests. Underline the form you hear, singular or plural.**

1. Do you have the (ticket, <u>tickets</u>) in your pocket?
2. Do you sell (candy, <u>candies</u>) in this store?
3. Put the (book, books) on the (shelf, shelves).
4. Where can I find the best clothing (store, stores)?
5. Are you buying the (gift, gifts) for your (friend, friends)?
6. Will you mail the (package, packages) and (letter, letters) for me please.
7. Where can I wash my (shirt, shirts)?
8. What (city, cities) are you going to visit on your trip?
9. Can you answer the (question, questions) in this lesson?
10. Please give my (greeting, greetings) to your (brother, brothers) and (sister, sisters).

F. One student asks the questions or makes the requests of Part E using either the singular or plural form. A second person will reply, indicating in the reply whether he or she heard the singular or plural form.

Do you have the tickets?
    Yes, they are in my pocket.
Do you have the ticket?
    Yes, I have it in my pocket.

LESSON   55

An arm and a leg:
Pronunciation of *a* and *an*

A. Listen and repeat. Notice that the word *an* is used before a vowel sound.

a nose   an eye   a leg   an arm

Form noun phrases. Use *a* or *an* with weak stress: a book, an egg.

foot	boy	ocean	ship	animal	umbrella
toe	girl	uncle	island	pig	coat
hand	child	man	exam	elephant	artist
ear	egg	woman	teacher	zoo	school bus
arm	map	apple	idea	envelope	infant

B. Which of these things will you find in an office? Which in a park? Form sentences. (*You'll find a desk in an office.*)

desk, chair, phone, flower, book, map, tree, rug, pen, lamp, eraser, bird, calendar, clock, flower, lake, zoo, map, bench, computer, path, swing, police officer, ant

C. Use a noun from the list a through j to complete the phrases 1 through 10. Use *a* or *an*. In rapid speech, the reduced form of *and* [ᵊn] is also used.

1. __a__ boy and __a__ girl   a. orange

2. _____ apple and _____ _____   b. girl

3. _____ man and _____ _____   c. leg

4. _____ stamp and _____ _____   d. Italian

5. _____ Greek and _____ _____   e. umbrella

6. _____ dog and _____ _____   f. woman

7. _____ raincoat and _____ _____   g. envelope

8. _____ adjective and _____ _____   h. cat

9. _____ house and _____ _____   i. apartment

10. _____ arm and _____ _____   j. adverb

D. Circle the phrase you hear: a, b, or c.

1. a. a boy and a girl   (b.) a boy and girl   c. boy and girl

2. a. a cup and a saucer   b. a cup and saucer   c. cup and saucer

3. a. a man and a woman   b. a man and woman   c. man and woman

4. a. a teacher and a student   b. a teacher and student   c. teacher and student

5. a. a stamp and an envelope   b. a stamp and envelope   c. stamp and envelope

6. a. a desk and a chair   b. a desk and chair   c. desk and chair

E. Use nouns from the two lists and form sentences. (*An apple is a fruit.*)

apple	animal	runner	instrument
baby	fruit	orchid	ship
man	vegetable	ocean liner	athlete
elephant	flower	bus	flower
rose	infant	frying pan	utensil
carrot	adult	scalpel	vehicle
pig	farm animal	pitchfork	farm tool

F. Match the synonyms and use them in a sentence. (*An exam is a test.*)

exam	chair	error	tram
artist	auto	painter	physician
doctor	streetcar	pharmacist	seat
mistake	druggist	test	car

G. Match the American and British terms for these things.

British	American
lift	truck
lorry	hood
hoarding	elevator
bonnet (of a car)	billboard

H. Form noun phrases. (*a dollar an hour*)

dollar/hour	dollar/yard	dollar/gallon	dollar/pound
penny/minute	penny/inch	penny/quart	penny/ounce

Now think of things that fit these costs. Form sentences. (*It costs a dollar an hour to park downtown./Parking costs a dollar an hour in that lot.*)

I. Tell what tools these workers use. Form sentences. (*A photographer uses a camera.*)

accountant	dentist	axe	hammer
artist	electrician	brush	knife
barber	woodcutter	camera	scissors
butcher	mechanic	computer	wirecutters
carpenter	photographer	drill	wrench

LESSON   56

The old and the new:
Pronunciation of *the*

A. Listen and repeat.

      the land   the air   the sea   the ocean

Notice the difference in pronunciation of *the* before a vowel and before a consonant.

    [thə]   the new   [thiʸ]   the old   the old and the new
    [thə]   the west   [thiʸ]   the east   the east and the west

B. Form noun phrases. Use *the* with weak stress before the words in the lesson on *a/an* (55, A).

    (the foot, the toe, the hand, the ear, and so on)

C. Repeat the words and phrases.

wall	on the wall	kitchen	in the kitchen
floor	on the floor	garage	in the garage
bedroom	in the bedroom	desk	under the desk
living room	in the living room	table	on the table

D. Ask where the following items are. A second student replies using the locations in Part C or any other suitable place.

Where's the sink in your house?
In the kitchen.
It's in the kitchen.
It's in the bathroom.

TV set	sofa	pots and pans	aspirin
rug	easy chairs	alarm clock	ladder
beds	bathtub	pens and pencils	electric meter
oven	wastebasket	piano	paint brushes
sink	phone	bread	lawnmower

E. Ask and answer questions about the things for sale.

How much are the cheese sandwiches?
They're one seventy-five.

Cheese and Salad Sandwiches

Cheddar Cheese	1.75
American Cheese	1.75
Swiss Cheese	1.75
Muenster Cheese	1.75
Provolone Cheese	1.75
Tuna Salad	2.50
Chicken Salad	2.50
Egg Salad	2.00
Chopped Chicken Liver	2.25
Jumbo Shrimp Salad	3.25

F. Ask or describe where certain buildings, landmarks, stores, and points of interest are in your city.

LESSON 57

She laughs and cries.

Pronunciation of third person singular verb form

As with noun plurals (see Lesson 54), the ending of the third person singular form of verbs depends on the final sound of the verb. The ending is [ᵊz] after [s], [z], [sh], [sh̵], [ch], or [j]. The ending is [s] after all other voiceless sounds (stops, laughs) and [z] after all other voiced sounds [runs, plays, carries).

A. Read each verb and pronounce the third person singular, present tense. (want–wants)

1. want	2. leave	3. watch	4. teach	5. ride
6. sleep	7. sell	8. land	9. sing	10. laugh
11. dig	12. cry	13. hear	14. run	15. close
16. breathe	17. smoke	18. race	19. come	20. take

B. Repeat the phrases. Note that verbs usually have strong stress. Listen to and imitate the rhythm.

watches TV	costs ten cents	washes the dishes
needs a book	rains every day	makes the beds
likes to swim	eats at noon	laughs and cries

C. Listen to these sentences read by your teacher or on tape and circle the form of the verb you hear.

1. leave
    (leaves)   at six o'clock
2. land
    lands   over there
3. sleep
    sleeps   all the time
4. wash
    washes   the dishes
5. play
    plays   baseball
6. run
    runs   to school every day
7. smoke
    smokes   a lot
8. speak
    speaks   English

D. Now form sentences. Use the subject *he* or *she*. (*He teaches English [in Brookmont School].*)

1. teach/English
2. drive/a taxi
3. write/books
4. bake/cakes
5. fix/bikes
6. read/love stories
7. sell/furniture
8. race/cars
9. manage/a restaurant

E. Play this memory game. Several students (six or seven or more) tell one thing that they do every day, such as eat breakfast or walk to school. After all the students have finished, the teacher selects someone in the class to recall what one particular student has said he or she does every day. For example:

(*Teacher:* What does Jean do every day?
Student: She takes care of her baby sister.)

Robert: I eat breakfast.
Lucy: I ride my bike.
Phil: I walk a mile.
Mary: I play records.
Jean: I take care of my baby sister.
George: I work in a store for two hours.
Teacher: Tom, what does Phil do every day?
Tom: He walks a mile.

F. Act out in pantomime different kinds of activities that you engage in on a regular basis. Swimming, rowing, mountain climbing, playing tennis, and reading are kinds of activities that can be acted out. Other students will guess what you are doing.

LESSON 58

You're right; I'm wrong.
Contractions of *am, is, are*

A. **Listen and repeat.**

he's [hiyz]   they're [ther]   I'm [aym]
she's [shiyz]   we're [wir]
it's [its]   you're [yur]

Using opposite adjectives with two contractions, form sentences like the example. (*They're famous; we're unknown.*)

he's	they're	tall	wrong	quiet	thin
I'm	you're	noisy	right	famous	late
we're	she's	short	early	unknown	fat

B. Answer the questions with a short affirmative statement. Use the information given. (*Am I right? Yes, you are. You're always right.*)

1.	Am I right?	a.	only fifteen dollars
2.	Is Joe old?	b.	seventy-five
3.	Is the lamp cheap?	c.	good friends
4.	Are you dressed?	d.	ready now
5.	Is Sally a baby?	e.	always right
6.	Are you and Joe friends?	f.	on the table
7.	Are the hamburgers ready?	g.	six months old

C. Form sentences. Use the contracted form of *is*. (*A ship's large. A boat's small.*)

1. a ship/a boat–large/small
2. a ball/a block–round/square
3. snow/fire–hot/cold
4. night/day–light/dark
5. snow/coal–white/black
6. a giraffe/a tree–an animal/a plant
7. an apple/a potato–a fruit/a vegetable
8. a piano/a balloon–heavy/light

D. Now form sentences with plural subjects. Use 're. (*Maria and Bob're writing a book.*)

1. Maria/Bob/writing a book
2. Pat/Ed/eating ice cream
3. Tom/Ann/learning English
4. Joyce/Liz/baking cookies
5. Sue/Ray/feeling fine
6. Julia/Frances/playing tennis
7. Ruth/Matt/wearing jeans
8. Richard/Susan/speaking Italian

E. Use the names of people you know (classmates, relatives, friends) and tell something they are doing at the present time.

(My father's building a boat. Tom's raising his hand. My parents're traveling in Japan. I'm sitting in class.)

LESSON 59

She isn't here.

The contraction -n't

A. **Listen to and repeat the contractions.**

isn't	
he isn't	she isn't
Tom isn't	it isn't

wasn't	
he wasn't	it wasn't
she wasn't	I wasn't

B. **Listen. Then repeat. First say [iz], then say [ᵊn]. Release the air through the nose after [iz]. The result should sound like [izᵊn].**

[iz] → [ᵊn]   [iz] → [ᵊn]   [iz] → [ᵊn]   [iz] → [ᵊn]

Now add the [t]. Form the stop for [t], but do not release it. Listen and repeat.

isn't	[iz] → [ᵊnt]	[iz] → [ᵊnt]	[iz] → [ᵊnt]	[iz] → [ᵊnt]
wasn't	[wəz] → [ᵊnt]	[wəz] → [ᵊnt]	[wəz] → [ᵊnt]	[wəz] → [ᵊnt]

C. **Listen to the questions and answers. Then repeat the answers.**

1. Is Tom here?   No, he isn't.   He isn't here now.
2. Is Sally home?   No, she isn't.   She isn't here.
3. Was it cold in January? No, it wasn't.   It wasn't cold then.
4. Were you at the bank?   No, I wasn't.   I wasn't there.

D. **Repeat the other contractions of *be, aren't* and *weren't*. Then listen to the questions and repeat the answers.**

Repeat	Listen	Repeat
you aren't	Am I late?	No, you aren't.
we aren't	Are we invited?	No, we aren't.
they aren't	Are they French?	No, they aren't.
you weren't	Was I correct?	No, you weren't.
we weren't	Were we on time?	No, we weren't.
they weren't	Were they talking?	No, they weren't.

E. **Listen to the questions. Then give a short answer and a statement from the list.** (*Is Mr. Ames old? No, he isn't. He's [only] twenty-seven.*)

1. Is Mr. Ames old?	a. in England
2. Is the sun shining now?	b. absent
3. Were you and Tom in France last year?	c. a classroom
4. Am I late?	d. twenty-seven
5. Is this the library?	e. early
6. Was Helen in class this morning?	f. last week
7. Was yesterday Heather's birthday?	g. cloudy today
8. Is the new promotion system a good one?	h. fair

F. **Repeat the contractions** *don't*, *doesn't*, **and** *didn't*. **In saying the contraction** *didn't*, **hold the tongue in position at the end of** *did* **and release the air through the nose for the [ᵊn] sound.**

didn't	[did] → [ᵊnt]	[did] → [ᵊnt]	[did] → [ᵊnt]	[did] → [ᵊnt]
doesn't	[dəz] → [ᵊnt]	[dəz] → [ᵊnt]	[dəz] → [ᵊnt]	[dəz] → [ᵊnt]
don't	[downt]	[downt]	[downt]	[downt]

G. **Listen to and repeat these sentences.**

I don't know.	He doesn't know.	She didn't know.
We don't work on Saturday.	She doesn't want it.	He didn't tell us.

H. **Read the sentences and listen to them. Then answer the questions about them.**

1. Mr. Ames didn't go to work today.
2. It didn't rain yesterday.
3. Mary doesn't have many friends.
4. Ted's sisters don't go to school.
5. Tom always walks to school.
6. Mrs. Ames doesn't feel well.
7. Billy doesn't like girls.
8. Mr. Oda doesn't speak Chinese.

I. **Ask yes-no questions about any subject—the weather, daily routine, celebrations, holidays, travel, or possessions. Try to ask questions that will probably require a negative reply.**

Is today your birthday? (No, it isn't.)
Did you study for four hours last night?
Is Sally the shortest girl in your class?
Do you drive an expensive car?

UNIT FIVE

Consonants

Consonant sounds are made by stopping the air at some point in the mouth ([b], [t]) or causing friction in the mouth ([s], [v]). Consonants can precede or follow the vowel of each syllable. You will practice the twenty-four consonant sounds of English as they contrast with each other (e.g., voiceless versus voiced, stops versus fricatives). Then you will do the consonant clusters that can begin and end English words.

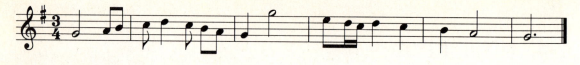

LESSON 60

Pea, tea, key, and so on:

All the consonants

A. Listen to and repeat these four words. They begin with consonant sounds that are similar to consonants found in many other languages, but they may not be exactly the same.

    bow [bow]   dough   Joe   go

On this facial diagram, the four consonants are placed in the position where the air is blocked. Say the four words once more.

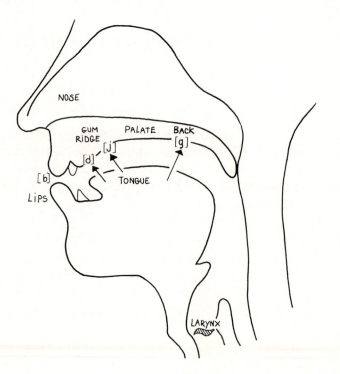

B. On this chart, all the English consonants are placed according to where the air is blocked or constricted in the mouth. Listen to and repeat all of the English consonants in words.

	Lips	*Teeth*	*Gum Ridge*	*Palate*	*Back*
Stopped Air	[p] pea [b] by		[t] tea [d] day	[ch] chew [j] joy	[k] key [g] go
Fricative Air	[f] fee [v] vow	[th] thigh [th] they	[s] say [z] zoo	[sh] she [sh] Asia	
Resonant Air	[m] my		[n] no [l] lie	[r] ray	[ŋ] king
Semivowels	[w] we			[y] you	

One consonant cannot be located on the chart: [h] how.

C. Say these phrases. Most of them are alliterative — both words begin with the same consonant sound.

1.	pen pal	2.	two toes	3.	cheap cheese	4.	can come
5.	by bus	6.	dark day	7.	just John	8.	go get
9.	fall fast	10.	say something	11.	she shows	12.	thin thighs
13.	very valuable	14.	zig zag	15.	Asian treasure	16.	then they
17.	my milk	18.	know nothing	19.	right road	20.	young king
21.	one way	22.	lie low	23.	yes, you	24.	how high

Use the above phrases in sentences.

6.   What a dark day! I thought it would be sunny today.
12.   She thinks that exercise will give her thin thighs.
17.   You're drinking my milk!

D. Read the paragraph aloud. Draw a circle around one example of each of the twenty-four English consonants, including [w], [y], and [h].

Don't you wish you could go to a place without crime, where people would help each other and follow the Golden Rule? There is just one thing about that vision of utopia. There wouldn't be anyone there.

LESSON 61

Look and listen:
The consonant [l]

A. Listen and repeat.

[l]	(Say the sound [l].)		
low	Our gas is low.	low number	The lake is low.
all	That's all.	all the time	That will be all.
yellow	It's yellow.	yellow balloon	The pillow is yellow.

Listen to and repeat the phrases.

Stop, look, and listen.   Look before you leap.

Listen for the sound [l]. Circle the corresponding number if you hear [l] in the word.

1.   2.   3.   4.   5.   6.   7.   8.   9.   10.

B. Change the sentences. Follow the examples.

1. The bell is loud. (It's a loud bell.)
2. The line is long.
3. The light is dim.
4. The pillow is yellow.
5. The lion cub was little.
6. The meal was lousy.
7. He had bad luck (His luck was bad.)
8. Linh has long legs.
9. Paul has a loose tooth.
10. That's a lazy fellow.
11. She's a tall lady.
12. It was a shallow lake.

C. Ask how these people feel. Answer with the appropriate adjective.

lucky/unlucky   lazy/lively   proud/foolish   well/ill

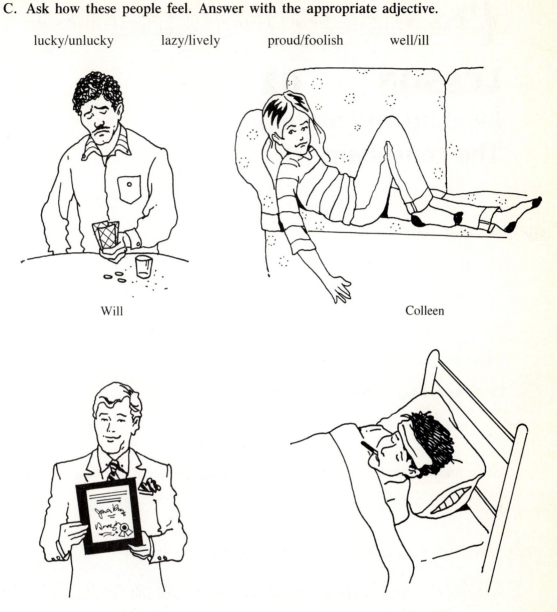

Will

Colleen

Mr. Lennox

Mrs. Lily

D. Tell someone to *look at*, *listen to*, *smell*, *taste*, or *feel* the things below. Then give a reason. *(Look at that lamp. It's broken.)*

lamp, lemon, lake, line, pillow, bell, girl, wall, milk

E. Tell what you will do in the future. Use some of these verbs or others. *(I will [I'll] learn a foreign language.)*

live, leave, let, look, learn, tell, sell, call, collect, follow, travel

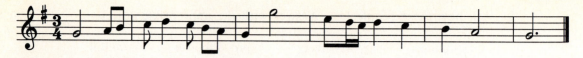

LESSON   62
Reading and writing:
The consonant [r]

A. Listen and repeat.

[r] (Say the sound [r].)

row	in a row	a row of books	right in a row
air	in the air	The air is hot.	Give me more air.
sorry	I'm sorry.	a sorry sight	We're very sorry.

Listen to and repeat these phrases.

right or wrong   reading and writing   rest and recreation

Listen for the sound [r]. Circle the corresponding number if you hear [r] in the word.

1.   2.   3.   4.   5.   6.   7.   8.   9.   10.

B. Form noun phrases. Then use three of your phrases and ask three questions.
(*rainy weather   Do you like rainy weather?*)

red	rubber	raw	weather	tire	rose
right	more	rear	rice	carrot	road
rainy	rich	wrong	reason	door	farmer

C. Name as many things and actions in the pictures as you can that begin with the sound [r]. (*roar, rest, rob, river, and so on.*)

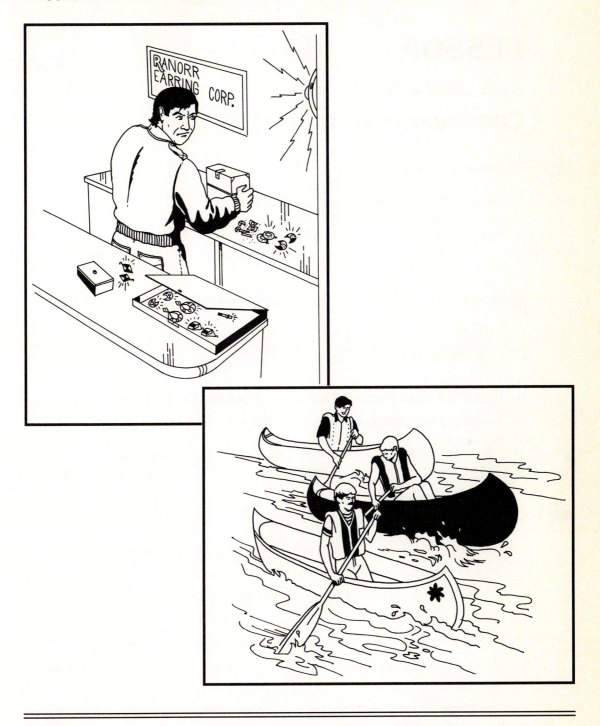

D. Make up a short story about a car race. Use some of these words.

race	driver	radio	run	roll	rain	ride	poor
car	tire	crash	hear	wear	far	sore	fair

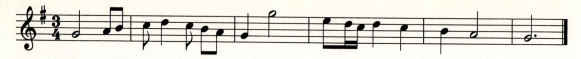

LESSON   63

Left and right:
Consonants [l] and [r]

A. Listen and repeat.

[l]	[r]	(Say the sounds [l] and [r].)	
low	row	Those bushes are low.	a row of low bushes
all	or	One for all and all for one.	It's all or none.
daily	dairy	Milking is a daily job at the dairy.	The dairy does it daily.

Listen to each word. Circle the consonant symbol that you hear.

1. [l] [r]   2. [l] [r]   3. [l] [r]
4. [l] [r]   5: [l] [r]   6. [l] [r]

B. Repeat the noun phrases. Then form sentences. Use an adjective that is opposite in meaning. *(The glass isn't empty. It's full.)*

1. an empty glass   2. a short road   3. the dirty car   4. a poor lady
5. a fast runner   6. a large school   7. a soft pillow   8. a short man

C. Read the paragaph and fill in *left* and *right*.

We drive on the _____ side of the road. The steering wheel is on the _____ side of our cars. We must pass another car on the _____, never on the _____. Most cars have automatic turn signals, but we may also signal with our _____ hand. In many places, we can turn _____ at a red light after stopping. On freeways, the _____ lanes are for faster traffic; slower traffic must keep in the _____ lane. In an emergency, we must pull off the road on the _____ and stop our car.

D. Repeat the color words. Then discuss the colors of things around you. *(The clouds are gray; Carrie's sweater is dark blue,* etc.)

purple	yellow	blue	white	gray	light	pink	silver
red	orange	green	black	brown	dark	maroon	gold

E. Listen to the sentences. Then circle a or b to complete the second sentences.

1. Don't stand in the (*lane/rain*).
   You'll get _____ .
   a. wet   b. hit

2. That's the (*long/wrong*) way to
   do the problem. Let me show
   you _____ way to do it.
   a. the right   b. the shorter

3. A ring fell into the (*glass/grass*).
   We'll get it back when we
   _____ it.
   a. mow   b. empty

4. The (*lock/rock*) is stuck. I can't
   _____ it.
   a. open   b. move

LESSON   64

Some young men:
Consonants [m], [n] and [ŋ]

A. Listen and repeat.

1. Mom
   Come home.
   Amy's coming.

2. noon
   not now
   Ann Nelson

3. long
   Let's sing.
   The bell's ringing.

some young men   Nan's winning.   The sun's going down.

B. Listen and repeat. The sounds [n] and [ŋ].

lawn	long	Our lawn is long, but not wide.	We have a long lawn.
thin	thing	This thing is too thin.	It's a very thin thing.

Listen to each word. Circle the sound you hear in it.

1. [n] [ŋ]   2. [n] [ŋ]   3. [n] [ŋ]
4. [n] [ŋ]   5. [n] [ŋ]   6. [n] [ŋ]

C. **Form noun phrases with the adjectives and nouns. Then use them in sentences.**
   (*a long pin   I found a long pin on the floor.*)

one	ten	thin		can	men	pin
long	strong	young		king	song	string

D. **Form sentences in the present perfect. Use a verb and a noun.** (*I've never won money in a lottery. He's known her name for a long time.*)

Verbs: draw, see, wear, know,   **Nouns:** animal, costume, monkey, money,
          sing, win   movie, name, poem, song

E. **Listen and repeat. The sounds [ŋ] and [ŋk].**

thing	think	That's a good thing, I think.	I think it's a good thing.
hang	Hank	Hank didn't hang up his coat.	Hang it up, Hank.

Listen to each word. Circle the sound you hear in it.

1. [ŋ] [ŋk]   2. [ŋ] [ŋk]   3. [ŋ] [ŋk]
4. [ŋ] [ŋk]   5. [ŋ] [ŋk]   6. [ŋ] [ŋk]

F. **Listen to the question. Then circle the correct answer, a or b.**

1. sung/sunk

   What have they _____?

   a. A battleship.

   b. a Christmas song.

2. sinner/singer

   Is he a terrible _____?

   a. Yes, he beats his wife.

   b. Yes, he can't hold a note.

3. sting (*hurt*)/stink (*smell*)

   Why does her hand _____?

   a. She bumped her elbow.

   b. She was handling spoiled fruit.

4. bang/bank

   How did the _____ scare you?

   a. They said I was overdrawn.

   b. It was very near and loud.

G. Listen to and repeat the pairs of words. Then listen to the sentences and write the missing words.

1. some/sub   That's _____ _____. A _____ is having

                  trouble.

2. Tammy/Tabby   _____ likes _____. _____ is a cat.

3. mad/man   A _____ _____. The _____ is very

                  _____.

4. hung/hug   He _____ his _____ on a hook. Did he

                  _____ his _____?

5. ringing/rigging   The _____ of the _____.

                  The _____ of the _____.

H. Listen to each word. Circle the sound you hear.

1. [m] [b]   2. [n] [d]   3. [ŋ] [g]
4. [m] [b]   5. [n] [d]   6. [ŋ] [g]

I. Form sentences. Use an adjective and noun in each.

flying   foggy   bigger   long | cigarette   morning   wagon   wing   eagle

LESSON   65

We hear you:
Consonants [y], [w] and [h]

A. Listen and repeat.

1. Yes, she's young.
   You're younger.
   A year ago yesterday

2. Don't watch Walter.
   Wait a week.
   The wood is wet.

3. It's hot here.
   Did you hear her?
   Who is he?

You have won.   We hear you.   Were you home?

B. Listen and repeat. The sounds [y] and [j].

yam	jam	I eat jam, but I don't like yams.	This yam is old.
yet	jet	Have you flown in our new jet yet?	No, not yet.

Listen to each word. Circle the sound you hear.

1. [y] [j]   2. [y] [j]   3. [y] [j]
4. [y] [j]   5. [y] [j]   6. [y] [j]

C. Form sentences. Use both words of each pair in the sentences.

1. yellow/jello   2. young/judge   3. year/journey   4. you/genius

D. Listen and repeat. Then circle the correct answer, a or b.

1. Yale/jail

Why did he go to _____ for four years?

a. He robbed a bank.

b. He was getting his law degree.

2. yam/jam

How much does this _____ cost?

a. It's $1.35 a jar.

b. They're about 15 cents each.

E. Listen and repeat. The sounds [w] and [v].

Wayne	vain	Wayne is very vain.	What a vain person Wayne is!
we'll	veal	Let's eat veal tonight.	OK, we'll have veal.

Form sentences. Use these names, verbs, and noun objects in several combinations.

Valerie	visit	victim	waiter
Wilma	watch	window	wine
Victor	wash	water	vacation
Walter	want	vase	vegetables

F. Listen and repeat. Then circle the correct answer, a or b.

1. wine/vine

Why did they throw out the _____?

a. It didn't taste good.

b. It wasn't growing well.

2. west/vest

Does this really belong in the _____?

a. No, it belongs in the suit.

b. No, it belongs in the east.

G. Listen and repeat. The sound [h] vs. no consonant.

hold	old	Hold on to your old coins.	This old pan won't hold water.
head	Ed	Ed hit his head.	I hurt my head, just like Ed did.

Repeat the phrases. Then use two of the phrases in sentences.

an old hat	a huge head	a hot hamburger	open house
an old apple	a huge orange	a hot evening	open arms

H. Fill in *all* or *half* in these sentences.

1. Hilda was working hard yesterday. Now _____ of her muscles hurt.

2. I can't give you _____ of my writing paper, but I can give you _____ of it.

3. In the American flag, _____ of the stars are white. Almost _____ of the stripes are white, too.

4. The election ended in a tie. _____ of the members voted for Hopper and _____ voted for Anderson.

I. Listen and repeat. Then circle the correct answer, a or b.

1. eat/heat

   Did you _____ the spinach?

   a. Yes, it's all gone now.

   b. Yes, it's hot now.

2. armed/harmed

   Was the police officer _____?

   a. No, he had no weapon.

   b. No, he's all right.

3. ale (*beer*)/hail (*ice*)

   Did you see the _____?

   a. Yes, it's in the refrigerator.

   b. Yes, it ruined some of my flowers.

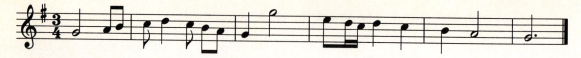

LESSON 66

Too, do, Sue, zoo:

Contrasts of voiceless and voiced consonants

A. Listen. Then repeat the pairs of words.

too	pie	came	chain	fan	thigh (*leg*)	Sue	shock
do	buy	game	Jane	van	thy (*your*)	zoo	Jacques

Listen to one word of each pair. Circle the word you hear. Now listen to and write the words you hear. Each sentence has two or three of the above words.

1. _____ _____ to the party late.

2. I'll _____ her a gold _____.

3. Some _____ spilled on her _____.

4. _____ you and _____ want to go to the _____?

5. _____ got a _____ from the toaster.

6. The team _____ to the _____ in a _____. Some _____ did _____.

B. Vowels are longer before voiced consonants than before unvoiced ones. Listen to these pairs of words. Then listen to one word of each pair and circle the one you hear.

write	writer	match	matches	rich	riches	bus	busing
ride	rider	Madge	Madge's	ridge	ridges	buzz	buzzing

C. Stop consonants in final position are often unreleased. Listen to all of these words. Then listen to one word of each pair and circle the one you hear.

back	rate	tap	hit	seat
bag	raid	tab	hid	seed

D. Listen to the question. Then circle the correct answer, a or b.

1. cap/cab

   How much did he pay for

   his _____?

   a. About $6.00

   b. About $15,000.

2. cot/cod

Where did you buy

the _____?

   a. At Marty's Furniture Store.

   b. At the fish market on 16th
      Street.

3. tack/tag

What are you going to do with

the _____?

   a. I'm going to hang it on the
      tree.

   b. I'm going to fasten this
      schedule to the wall with it.

E. **Have one student use one of the words of each pair in asking a question. Another student answers the question with a full sentence.** (*Do you ever bet on football games? No, I never bet at all.*)

1. bet/bed	2. rope/robe	3. life/live (adj)	4. race/raise
5. matter/madder	6. back/bag	7. Mable/maple	8. precedent/president

---

F. **Where do you hear the sound? Write B (for beginning of the word) or E (for end of the word).** (*1. beep [p] is at the end of the word.*)

1. [p] ___E___   2. [b] _____   3. [k] _____

4. [g] _____   5. [t] _____   6. [d] _____

7. [s] _____   8. [z] _____   9. [f] _____

10. [j] _____

G. **Fill in the blanks with words from the lists.**

1. He _____ a hole and buried the dead _____.

    tuck   tug   duck   dug

2. Billy _____ 50 cents for the _____.

    pate   paid   bait   bayed

3. The _____ driver wore a black _____.

    cap   cab   gap   gab

H. **Repeat the pairs of words. Then listen to the question and give a logical answer.**

1. goat   coat   Is this your pretty white _____?

2. cap   cab   How much did the _____ cost you?

3. time   dime   Do you have the _____?

4. writing riding   I didn't understand. Did you say you spent your time _____?

5. rope   robe   Where did you buy the red _____ ?

6. cheer   jeer   Why did the crowd _____ the basketball player?

7. joking   choking   Were you _____ ?

8. fan   van   Where's a good place to buy a _____ ?

LESSON 67

First, thirst, sell, shell:

Contrasts among fricatives

A. Listen to the pairs of words, then repeat them. Next listen to one word of each pair. Circle the word you hear.

first	thumb	sell	van	then	Caesar
thirst	some	shell	than	Zen	seizure

Listen to the sentences and fill the blanks with the words you hear.

1. My friend is going to _____ his _____ .

2. Do you want to _____ those _____ ? They're prettier _____ mine.

3. _____ I hurt my thumb. _____ I broke my wrist.

4. I'm _____ . I would like _____ water, please.

B. First repeat. Then listen to and write the last word that you hear.

1. four   Thor   sore   shore   _____

2. laugh   lath (*stick*)   lass   lash (*whip*)   _____

3. clove (*spice*)   clothe   close   _____

4. bathe (*wash*)   bays   beige (*brown*)   _____

C. Listen to each word. Circle the sound you hear.

1. [th]   [t̶h̶]   2. [f]   [v]   3. [z]   [s̶h̶]

4. [s]   [z]   5. [sh]   [s̶h̶]   6. [s]   [sh]

📼   **D. Listen to the question. Choose the correct answer, a or b.**

1. C/Z

   What letter comes after _____
   in the alphabet?

   a. "D"

   b. None. It's the last letter of the
      alphabet.

2. racer/razor

   What makes a good _____?

   a. It has to be very sharp.

   b. She has to be very fast.

3. fan/van

   How much did the _____
   cost?

   a. $11.00.

   b. $11,000.

📼   **E. A few nouns ending with [th] have verb forms that end with [th̶]. The vowel sound also changes. Repeat the words and fill in the blanks.**

bath	breath	mouth (n)	tooth
bathe	breathe	mouth (v)	teethe

Our baby took his first _____ on April tenth. That's his birthday. He was

born without _____. He'll begin to _____ in about six months. He can

_____ a lot of sounds, but speech won't come from his _____ for about

a year. Our baby loves his _____. We _____ him about twice a week.

And we check his _____ every night.

F. Repeat the names and occupations. Then form sentences. (*Vivian is now a famous business woman.*)

Names:
Gigi, Heather, Rose, Vivian

Occupations:
business woman, clothing designer, movie star,
weather reporter

G. Repeat the names and sports terms. Then form sentences. (*Keith competed in the marathon race.*)

Names:
Chris, Josh, Jeff, Keith

Sports:
athlete, discus throw, javelin, shot put, decathalon,
hurdles, marathon, track and field events

H. **Read each sentence. Then form a new sentence using *with*.**

1. Some houses have fireplaces. (Houses with fireplaces sell for more money.)
2. Some farms have modern equipment.
3. Some fish have no eyes.
4. Some vans have beds in them.
5. Some caves have ancient pictures in them.
6. Some movies have a lot of violence.
7. Some love stories have a sad ending.

LESSON 68

Day, they, chew, shoe:
Contrasts of stop and fricative consonants

A. **Repeat the underlined words and phrases. The sounds [t] versus [th] and [d] versus [t̶h̶].**

This tin is thin.   Dan is taller than me.
  It's thin tin.   But Kim's taller than Dan.

Sam bet Beth.   They said they were coming the next day.
  Beth bet him a dollar.   But that wasn't the day they came.

B. **Listen to each word. Circle the sound you hear.**

1. [t] [th]   2. [t] [th]   3. [d] [t̶h̶]
4. [t] [th]   5. [d] [t̶h̶]   6. [d] [t̶h̶]

C. **Form noun phrases with *that* and use them in sentences with *too*. Begin your sentences with *I think*. (*I think that dog is too thin.*)**

dog, tie, door, desk, tire, teacher, doctor, tin

D. Listen to the question. Then circle the correct answer, a or b.

1. boot/booth

   How does a _____ protect
   you?

   a. It keeps the sun and rain off
      of you.

   b. It keeps your feet dry.

2. team/theme

   Which _____ won
   first place?

   a. The New York Yankees.

   b. The one Penny wrote.

3. ladder/lather

   What happened to the

   _____?

   a. It got cold.

   b. It broke.

4. day/they

   Will _____ come soon?

   a. Yes, it's almost dawn.

   b. Yes, they'll be here in twenty
      minutes.

E. Repeat the words and sentences. The sounds [ch] versus [sh] and [j] versus [s̶h̶].

That dog's chewing my shoes!
Butch was hiding in the bushes.
Did they catch the thief with the cash?

Major George Pledger was born in Asia.
The major was born in Malaysia.
Major Pledger? It's a pleasure to meet you.

F. Listen to each word. Circle the sound that you hear in it.

1. [ch] [sh]   2. [ch] [sh]   3. [j] [s̶h̶]
4. [ch] [sh]   5. [j] [s̶h̶]   6. [j] [s̶h̶]

**G. Form sentences. Use both words in each sentence. (*I choose carefully when I shop for
clothes.*)**

1. choose/shop
2. chair/cushion
3. fresh/peach
4. which/wish
5. show/china
6. Asian/agent

H. Listen to the question. Then circle the correct answer, a or b.

1. ditch/dish

   Is the _____ still wet?

   a. Yes, dry it with a towel.

   b. Yes, pump the water out.

2. chip/ship

   What is that kind of

   _____ used for?

   a. It's used in modern computers.

   b. It carries bananas.

3. watching/washing

   What are you _____ there?

   a. A nature program.

   b. Jeans and colored things.

4. pledger/pleasure

   Is Doug really a big _____?

   a. Yes, he always gives a lot of money.

   b. Yes. I always enjoy seeing him.

I. The sound [p] versus [f] and [b] versus [v]. Listen and repeat.

Puns are fun.
Your shirt cuff is in your coffee cup.

My! These berries are very sweet!
Sybil's a civil service worker.

Listen to each word. Circle the sound that you hear.

1. [p] [f]   2. [p] [f]   3. [b] [v]
4. [p] [f]   5. [b] [v]   6. [b] [v]

J. Form noun phrases with *fine*. Then tell what you think a fine one of each thing is like. (*A fine apple. A fine apple is shiny, red, and sweet.*)

   apple, ship, picture, pillow, pony, pool

K. Listen to the question. Then circle the correct answer, a or b.

1. pan/fan

   What does a _____ do?

   a. It holds water.

   b. It keeps you cool in hot weather.

2. boat/vote

   When will the next _____ come?

   a. It'll be held in a week.

   b. It'll dock next week.

3. curb/curve

   Can I park on the _____?

   a. No, park where the road is straight.

   b. No, park on the street.

4. cap/calf

   Did the farmer get a new _____?

   a. Yes, he's going to build a herd with it.

   b. Yes, he wears it everywhere.

L. Repeat words with the voiceless stopped consonants and fricative sounds.
Form sentences. Use two or more words from each group. (*That's Doris over there—the tall, thin young woman.*)

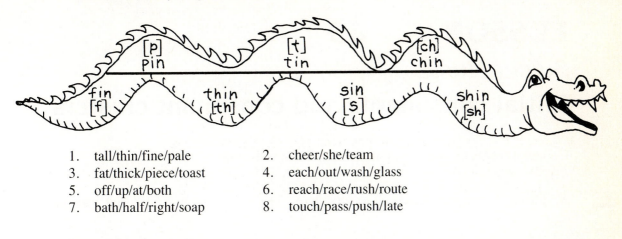

1. tall/thin/fine/pale
2. cheer/she/team
3. fat/thick/piece/toast
4. each/out/wash/glass
5. off/up/at/both
6. reach/race/rush/route
7. bath/half/right/soap
8. touch/pass/push/late

M. Repeat words with the voiced stopped consonants and fricative sounds.

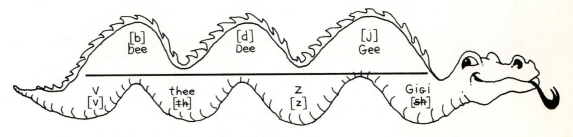

Form sentences. Use both words. (*He was born in a country village.*)

1. born/village
2. trouble/travel
3. job/live
4. daughter/there
5. cheese/bread
6. please/page
7. dozen/zebra
8. need/use
9. lathe/wood
10. meadow/desert
11. giant/zany
12. magic/reason
13. zipper/Germany
14. region/erosion
15. governor/gubernatorial

LESSON 69

Sweet Music

Initial consonants and consonant clusters

English words begin with no, one, two, or three consonants.

A. Listen and repeat. Read across the chart. The first word has no initial consonant.

No Initial Consonant: old		*Initial [y]:* you		*Initial [w]:* we		*Initial [r]:* row		*Initial [l]:* lie	
[g]	go		—	[gw]	Gwen	[gr]	grow	[gl]	glad
[k]	key	[ky]	cute	[kw]	quiet	[kr]	cry	[kl]	climb
[sk]	sky	[sky]	skewer	[skw]	square	[skr]	scratch		—
[b]	bee	[by]	beauty		—	[br]	brown	[bl]	blue
[p]	pie	[py]	pure		—	[pr]	prove	[pl]	play
[sp]	spoon	[spy]	spurious		—	[spr]	spring	[spl]	splash
[d]	do	*[dy]	due	[dw]	Duane	[dr]	draw		—
[t]	too	*[ty]	tune	[tw]	twenty	[tr]	tree		—
[st]	stay	*[sty]	stew		—	[str]	strong		—
[v]	vote	[vy]	view		—		—		—
[f]	fine	[fy]	few		—	[fr]	free	[fl]	fly
[th]	thing		—	[thw]	thwart	[thr]	three		—
[s]	see	*[sy]	suit	[sw]	swim		—	[sl]	slow
[sh]	show		—		—	[shr]	shrink		—
[h]	he	[hy]	huge	*[hw]	white		—		—
[m]	me	[my]	music		—		—		—
[n]	no	*[ny]	news		—		—		—

Common words also begin with these sounds:

[z]	zoo	[th]	they	[ch]	chew	[j]	job
[sn]	snow	[sm]	smile	[sf]	sphere		

*Many English speakers do not pronounce the [y] or [h] in these words.

B. Some words have [y] after another consonant sound. Use a word from the [y] column of the chart to answer each question.

1. What are we listening to? (We're listening to some music.)
2. What word is the opposite of *very small*?

   3. Why do people sometimes buy water at the store?
   4. Do you want to make a lot of mistakes on a test?
   5. What do you think of baby's shoes?
   6. Why do people stop their car there and look around?

C. **Some words have [w] after another consonant. Use a word from the [w] column of the chart to answer each question.**

   1. What is a boy's name in the column?
   2. How old do you think he might be?
   3. What color is his hair?
   4. Is he a noisy person?
   5. What does he do every weekend?
   6. What shape is his classroom?

D. **Some words have [r] after another consonant. Use a word from the [r] column of the chart to answer each question.**

   1. What season is May Day in?
   2. Does everyone have to buy tomatoes?
   3. How much did you pay for this sample?
   4. What color are her eyes?

E. **Some words have [l] after another consonant. Use a word from the [l] column to answer each question.**

   1. What color is the sky?
   2. What do all children like to do?
   3. Does everyone walk fast?

F. **Repeat the words:**

black	dress	sleep	throat
blue	drive	street	train
dream	pretty	strong	travel

Now fill in the blanks with appropriate words from the list.

   1. The movie <u>King Kong</u> was filmed in _____ and white.

   2. The opposite of weak is _____.

   3. I never take planes. I always _____ by _____.

   4. Do you know how to _____ a car?

   5. John has a cold and a sore _____.

   6. My address is 2126 24th _____.

   7. I _____ eight hours every night but I never _____.

   8. The young lawyer was wearing a very _____ _____ _____.

G. Repeat the words. Then fill in the blanks with words from the list.

squeeze	splinter	stranger
shrink	thread	scream

1. I washed my new shirt. I hope it didn't _____.

2. Let's have orange juice this morning. Will you _____ a few oranges, please?

3. If you're going to sew on buttons, you'll need a needle and _____.

4. I've never met that man. He's a complete _____.

5. She was terrified, but was unable to _____.

6. My finger's sore. I think I have a _____ in it.

H. Form noun phrases with the adjectives and nouns. Use them in sentences.
(beautiful view   They have a beautiful view from their window.)

blue	glad	strong		beauty	fly	spring
brown	green	sweet		bread	glass	square
clean	huge	three		cloth	grass	string
cute	proud	true		cross	music	tree
dry	pure	twenty		cube	plane	view
few	slow	beautiful		dress	quarter	musician

LESSON   70

A simple symbol:
Medial consonants and consonant clusters

A. Say each consonant sound in final position and medial position.

stop/stopping	write/writer	time/timing
rub/rubber	ride/riding	sing/singer
off/offer	lock/locker	witch/witches
love/loving	log/logger	wash/washer

B. Say each pair of words. Then listen as one of the words is spoken again. Circle that word.

1. riding/writing	2. logger/locker	3. ringer/rigor
4. Mabel/maple	5. fuzzy/fussy	6. aloe/arrow
7. rival/rifle	8. edging/etching	9. glazier/glacier

C. **Listen to and repeat words that have [t] or [d] between vowels. Then fill in the blanks with words from the list and read the sentences aloud.**

butter/button	lattice/Latin	woody/wooden	redder/redden
kitty/kitten	subtle/Sutton	ladle/laden	hiding/Haydn

1. He spilled _____ on his shirt.
2. The _____ on my coat is loose. I hope I don't lose it.
3. A _____ will come to you if you say, "Here, _____ _____."
4. He was embarrassed, and his face got _____ and _____.
5. I can't find Jimmy. Do you think he's _____?

D. **Repeat the underlined words and sentences. These medial clusters have [r] and [l].**

1. Ardis wasn't at the party.
2. Archie was a sergeant in the army.
3. Martha Larson married Marvin Marshall.
4. This is the album of our Alpine trip.
5. The butler's name was Dudley.
6. Wilga welcomed the guests warmly.

E. **Answer with a full sentence. Add -*ly* to one of the adjectives in the list and form an adverb.**

1. How does he sleep? (He sleeps soundly.)
2. How does the car run?
3. How did the soldiers fight?
4. How did the actor dress?
5. How did the president speak?

brave	quick	smooth
clear	rich	soft
fierce	rough	sound
frank	sharp	strange

F. **Repeat the pairs of words. The medial clusters have [m], [n] and [ŋ].**

1. symbol/simple	2. Dempsey/Ramsey	3. Denzel/pencil
4. drinker/finger	5. Ridgemont/Richmond	6. Jenner/center
7. mentioned/danger	8. window/winter	9. Houghton/mountain
10. Disney/Passner		

Now select three pairs of words from the list above and form three statements or questions using them. (*Jenner was the regular center on our basketball team.*)

G. Read the names of these football players and former players. Then compare their ages. Use *older than*, *younger than*, or *the same age as*. (*Pitman is older than Cushman.*)

Pitman, 45	Beckman, 26	Hoffman, 32	Crossman, 77	Fineman, 21
Goodman, 81	Hagman, 61	Cushman, 39	Wiseman, 29	Pullman, 32

H. Repeat these sets of words. The medial clusters have stops or [s] or [z].

1. Edsel/pretzel
2. Bugsie/taxi
3. whispered/husband
4. risky/exit
5. captain/napkin
6. Edgar/Rutgers
7. Pitkin/Redken
8. Clifton/doctor/Ogden

Now listen to the questions and answer them.

1. Who ate the pretzels? (Edsel did.)
2. Who took a taxi home?
3. Who did Jane whisper to?
4. What is risky to use?
5. What does the captain need?
6. Who's going to Rutgers College?
7. Who sells Redken products?
8. What is the name of the doctor who practices in Ogden?

I. Read the names. Then complete the sentences. Use any name from the list and add *-ful* to one of the nouns in parentheses to form an adjective.

Jepson	Gibson
Matson	Hudson
Jackson	Gregson
Leffson	Dodgeson
Wilson	Carson
Johnson	Simpson

1. Mr. Hudson is a careful worker. (care, skill)

2. Mrs. _____ got rid of the _____ insects. (dread, harm)

3. Mr. _____ is very _____ about his health. (doubt, thank)

4. Mrs. _____ spent a _____ night. (rest, wake)

5. Miss _____ had a _____ operation. (help, pain)

6. Mr. _____ is a _____ person. (peace, truth)

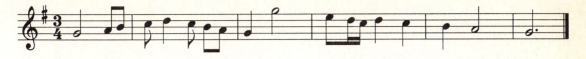

LESSON 71

Drink your milk

Final consonants and consonant clusters

English words end with no, one, two, or three consonants, not counting words that have a plural or past suffix.

A. Listen and repeat. Read across. The first word has no final consonant.

No Final Consonant: go, see		[r] + Final Consonant		[l] + Final Consonant		Nasal + Final Consonant	
[k]	ache	[rk]	mark	[lk]	milk	[ŋk]	ink
[g]	egg	[rg]	morgue	—		—	
[p]	hope	[rp]	sharp	[lp]	help	[mp]	camp
[b]	rob	[rb]	garb	[lb]	bulb	—	
[t]	eight	[rt]	art	[lt]	belt	[nt]	ant
[d]	add	[rd]	hard	[ld]	gold	[nd]	and
[ch]	match	[rch]	march	[lch]	welch	[nch]	inch
[j]	edge	[rj]	large	[lj]	bulge	[nj]	change
[f]	if	[rf]	scarf	[lf]	shelf	[mf]	triumph
[v]	of	[rv]	carve	[lv]	solve	—	
[th]	math	[rth]	north	[lth]	health	[nth]	month
[t̶h̶]	breathe	—		—		—	
[s]	us	[rs]	horse	[ls]	else	[ns]	dance
[z]	as	[rz]	Mars	—		[nz]	lens
[sh]	wish	[rsh]	marsh	[lsh]	Welsh	—	
[s̶h̶]	beige	—		—		—	
[m]	am	[rm]	arm	[lm]	film	—	
[n]	in	[rn]	corn	[ln]	kiln	—	
[ŋ]	sing	—		—		—	
[l]	all	[rl]	Carl	—		—	
[r]	or	—		—		—	

Common words also end with these sounds.

[kt]	act	[ks]	ax	[sk]	desk	[ts]	blitz
[ŋkt]	extinct	[ŋks]	jinx	[sp]	wasp	[rts]	quartz
[pt]	adapt	[ps]	collapse	[st]	fast	[lts]	waltz
[mpt]	tempt	[mps]	glimpse	[nst]	against	[ft]	lift

B. Some words end with [r] and another consonant. Use a word from the [r] column to answer each question.

1. What vegetable is often served with a meal?
2. Is Chicago in the South?
3. Jane draws very well. What should she study?
4. How did Jim hurt himself?
5. What's Mary wearing around her neck?
6. What does the teacher do with tests?
7. Is that a star in the sky?
8. What is the baby's name?

C. Some words ends with [l] and another consonant. Use a word from the [l] column to answer each question.

1. Why doesn't this light work?
2. What did Mrs. Fay buy at the grocery store?
3. What's that ring made of?
4. Where's the sugar?
5. Why don't you smoke any more?
6. What nationality is he?

D. Some words end with [m], [n], or [ŋ] and another consonant. Use a word from the nasal column to answer each question.

1. What shall we do on the weekend?
2. How long is it till spring?
3. Is this a good camera?
4. How long is this line? ─────────────
5. Do you have a red pen?
6. Is that a fly?

E. Form sentences using these verbs and objects. *(I can't lift this box.)*

act	dust	park		bank	bus	desk	maid
ask	fix	send		belt	camp	film	milk
change	help	sort		bench	card	gold	part
drink	lift	want		box	corn	horse	shelf

 UNIT SIX

Sentence Stress and Rhythm

The sentence rhythm created by the pattern of stressed and unstressed syllables results in the reduction (or unstressing) of many one-syllable grammar words. In this section you will practice the reduced forms of articles, pronouns, prepositions, and conjunctions. Then you will practice the stressing of sentences in which no particular word is being emphasized. Finally, you will learn how to emphasize or contrast any word in a sentence.

LESSON   72

Sooner or later:
Reduced forms

Rhythm in English is the alternation of strongly and weakly stressed syllables. In English colloquial conversation, there are more weakly stressed syllables than strongly stressed ones. Many of these weakly stressed syllables are reduced forms of some of the most common grammar words of one syllable, such as *a, the, and, or, are, can, of,* and *his.* In a reduced form, the vowel sound usually becomes [ə], called *schwa.*

 A. Listen and repeat. In informal writing, *and* **is sometimes written** *'n'.*

	Full Form	*Reduced Form*
and	[ænd]/[æn]	[ən]/[ənd]
	Jim and I	Jim 'n' I
	cream and sugar	cream 'n' sugar
	eat and drink	eat 'n' drink

	Full Form	*Reduced Form*
or	[ɔr]	[ər]
	Jim or Ted	Jim or Ted
	salt or pepper	salt or pepper
	one or two	one or two

Repeat these phrases.

knife and fork   coming and going   sooner or later

work and play   sink or swim   June or July   hungry and tired

B. Ask the model question. Reply, using two appropriate items from the lists.

(*What do shoe stores sell? They sell shoes and sandals.*)

shoe store	medicine	sandals
drugstore	shoes	vegetables
sports store	dresses	envelopes
post office	fruits	candy
clothing store	stamps	suits
grocery store	tennis balls	golf clubs

C. Ask an *or* **question. Use either two or three foods. Reply as indicated.**

(*Would you like (Do you want) coffee or tea?/Would you like coffee, tea, or milk? I'd like milk, please.*)

coffee	tea	milk
fruit	cake	ice cream

toast	bread	rolls
rice	potatoes	noodles
peas	carrots	tomatoes
chicken	fish	steak

D. Listen to and repeat the phrases which use reduced forms of the articles.

a	[ə]	read a book	the	[thə]	read the book
an	[ən]	eat an egg	some	[səm]	eat some bread

E. Form phrases with *and*. Use the reduced form of *and* [ən] and the reduced form of the words in parentheses.

1. (a) book/pencil (a book 'n' a pencil)
2. (the) man/woman
3. (an, some) egg/coffee
4. (an) apple/orange
5. (the) book/play
6. (an, a) arm/leg

LESSON   73

Add 'n' subtract:

Reduced forms and rhythm

A. Listen and repeat. The reduced forms of *is* and *are* (which include the contractions *'s* and *'re*) are very common.

	Full Form		*Reduced Forms and Contractions*	
are	[ar]		[ər]	
	The men are busy.		The men're busy.	
	When are they coming?		When're they coming?	
	[iz]	[əz]	[s]	[z]
is	Pat is here.	Pat is here.	Pat's here.	
	Pam is here.	Pam is here.		Pam's here.
	Lunch is ready.	Lunch is ready.		

There is no contraction, only a reduced form of *is* and *are* after a word that ends in a sound like *s, z, ch,* or *sh*. Listen.

[əz] Her face is red.   [ər] The buses are late.   [əz] Joyce is his daughter.

B. Ask a question-word question. Use these question words: *when, where, how, what time,* and *why.* Choose an appropriate reply from the phrases below.

(*When are you going? Tomorrow morning.*)

to the airport
tomorrow morning
to catch a plane
at six o'clock
by bus

C. Form sentences. Use *is* or *are.* (*The buses are full.*)

1. The buses   a. blue
2. Alice   b. very high
3. Paris   c. in France
4. The prices   d. full
5. The sandwiches   e. biting
6. The fish   f. in Europe
7. Our class   g. ready
8. France   h. my sister
9. Her dress   i. in Room 6

D. These phrases and sentences all have the same rhythm. Each has one or more reduced words. Listen to the phrases and sentences, then repeat them.

DÁ DǍ DǍ DÁ   DÁ DǍ DǍ DÁ

What is your name?   What do you want?
John is my friend.   Do it again.

DÁ DA DA DÁ   DÁ DA DA DÁ

open and close   Turn to the right.
doctor and nurse   Call me tonight.

E. Listen to the following phrases and sentences. Do they all have the same DÁ DA DA DÁ rhythm? Or are some of them different? Mark whether they have the same DÁ DA DA DÁ rhythm or a different rhythm.

First listen to two model sentences.

DÁ DǍ DǍ DÁ

Where is the book?
Call me tonight.

1. Where do you work?
2. doctor and nurse
3. add and subtract
4. John, Mark, and Jim
5. Polish your shoes.
6. He's a good man.

Listen to the rhythm again.

DÁ dȧ dȧ DÁ

	1	2	3	4	5	6
Same						
Different						

	7	8	9	10	11	12	13	14
Same								
Different								

F. **Listen to and repeat the sentences. Then add one or two sentences of your own using the same rhythm.**

1. I need a book.   (two strong stresses)
   I want some stamps.
   She bought the dress.

The basic rhythm of a sentence is established by the beat of the strongly stressed syllables. Additional weakly stressed syllables can be added without disturbing the basic rhythm. Listen and repeat these sentences. Then add one or two of your own.

2. I needed a book.   (two strong stresses)
   I wanted some paper.
   She's buying a sweater.

Many bumper stickers are made on the model of "I'd rather be sailing." Design one that shows your own interest. (*I'd rather be swimming.*)

3. I'd rather be sailing.

G. **Sentences with different grammatical forms may have the same sentence rhythm. Listen to and repeat these sentences which have three strong stresses, and form one or two of your own that have the same basic rhythm.**

1. John married Sue.
   Anne bought some stamps.
   George wanted to stay.

2. Helen was born in England.
   Freddy is now a hero.
   Betty agreed to tell'im.

H. Listen to these short poems. Tap your finger at each strong stress.

THREE STORMS

1. *On the Beach*

Clouds take over,
The rain's begun.
Beach umbrellas
Pick up and run.

2. *In the Town*

It was a hot wind, bright sun
Frozen yogurt kind of day.
Until the black clouds and slanting rain
Said what they had to say.

3. *On the Way Home*

The wind blew; the sky grew black.
It was difficult for me to see.
Did I run into the rainstorm,
Or the rainstorm run into me?

By Harriet Sheeler

MODERN TECHNOLOGY

If you'd told me twenty years ago,
I would've said, "It isn't so.
You can cook in a box that never gets hot
But heats the food to the right degree."
I would've said, "You're kidding me."
But I own one now. Oh, the time it saves,
This magical servant, the microwave.

By Harriet Sheeler

LESSON 74

Are ya ready?
Subject pronouns

Reduced forms of subject pronouns are very common in speech at normal speed. Note that the combination of *be* + subject pronoun is commonly spoken as one word (is it = [**izit**]).

	Full	*Reduced*	
I	[ay]	[aʸ]	[a]
we	[wiy]	[wiʸ]	
you	[yuw]	[yu]	[yᵊ]
they	[they]	[~~the~~ʸ]	
he	[hiy]	[iʸ]	
she	[shiy]	[shiʸ]	
it	[it]	[it]	

A. Listen to the sentences. First the full forms are used; then the same sentences are spoken with reduced forms and weak stress. The reduced forms of *he* and *you* are sometimes spelled *'e* and *ya* in informal writing.

Slow, Careful Speech				*Faster Speech*	
he	Is he . . . ?	[iz hiy]	Is he here?	[iziʸ]	Is 'e here?
you	Are you . . . ?	[ar yuw]	Are you ready?	[aryᵊ]	Are ya ready?
I	Am I . . . ?	[æm ay]	Am I early?	[æmaʸ]	Am I early?
we	Are we . . . ?	[ar wiy]	Are we late?	[arwiʸ]	Are we late?
they	Are they . . . ?	[ar ~~they~~]	Are they coming?	[artheʸ]	Are they coming?
it	Is it . . . ?	[iz it]	Is it raining?	[izit]	Is it raining?

B. Reduced pronoun forms are also common with the past tense of *be*, especially in questions.

Was he . . . ?	[wəz hiy]	Was he there?
Was it . . . ?	[wəz it]	Was it you?
Were you . . . ?	[wᵊr yuw]	Were you home?

[wəziʸ]	Was 'e there?
[wəzit]	Was it you?
[wᵊryᵊ]	Were ya home?

📼   C. **Now fill in the blanks with the form of *be* and the subject pronoun you hear.**

1. <u>Is</u> <u>she</u> home?   5. ___ ___ tall?   9. When ___ ___ going?

2. ___ ___ sick?   6. ___ ___ late?   10. What ___ ___ doing?

3. ___ ___ in school?   7. ___ ___ there?   11. ___ ___ on time?

4. ___ ___ coming?   8. ___ ___ hungry?   12. Where ___ ___ sleeping?

📼   D. **Listen to the subject pronouns with the auxiliaries *do*, *does*, and *did*. *Do* + *you* is generally pronounced [dəyᵊ] in rapid speech and sometimes represented in writing as *d'ya*.**

you	Do you . . . ?	[dúw yúw]	Do you swím?	[dǝyᵊ]	D'ya swím?
he	Does he . . . ? Did he . . . ?	[dǝz hiy] [did hiy]	Does he teach? Did he go?	[dǝziʸ] [didiʸ]	Does'e teach? Did'e go?
it	Does it . . . ? Did it . . . ?	[dǝz it] [did it]	Does it work? Did it rain?	[dǝzit] [didit]	Does it work? Did it rain?

Did + *you* is most often pronounced [didjᵊ] and often written *didja.*

Did you . . . ?   [díd yúw]   Did you téll him?   [dídjᵊ]   Didja téll'im?

📼   E. **Listen. *Did you* 'n' Tom go? Where *did you* see'im? When *did you* arrive? Fill in the auxiliary and pronoun you hear.**

1. <u>Did</u> <u>he</u> go?   4. Where ___ ___ work?   7. When ___ ___ call?

2. ___ ___ swim?   5. ___ ___ know?   8. Who ___ ___ tell?

3. ___ ___ teach?   6. ___ ___ come?   9. Where ___ ___ go?

F. **Ask questions about people in your class, friends, relatives, or about some thing or place. First identify the person or thing you are asking about with a sentence such as:**

I want to ask you about (your sister June, your hometown).

or

I've always wondered about (your grandfather).

Then ask a yes-no question using *do*, *does*, or *did* and a subject pronoun. Ask about any activity, interest, hobby, travel, daily routine, or about the weather.

1. I want to ask you about the weather in your country.
   Does it snow in the winter?
2. I like your new car.
   Does it get good mileage?
3. I met your friends Joe and Martha.
   Did you go to school with them?

G. Listen to the word and the question using the word. Then give an affirmative short answer. These questions and answers use *be*. (*Yes, he is*.)

1. tired 2. hungry 3. late 4. ready 5. hot 6. thirsty 7. cold 8. early

H. These questions and answers use *do* and *does*. Again give short answers to the questions that use the word or phrase. (*Yes, I do*.)

1.	know John	2.	swim	3.	go to school
4.	speak some English	5.	snow	6.	play tennis

I. Listen to the statements. Then show surprise by responding with rising intonation.

1. Mary is my sister. She is?
2. We are late. We are?
3. John is sick. _____?
4. _____ _____?
5. _____ _____?
6. _____ _____?

7. Tom drives a taxi. He does?
8. They speak Chinese. They do?
9. _____ _____?
10. _____ _____?
11. _____ _____?
12. _____ _____?

LESSON   75
What's 'er name?
Possessive modifiers

A. Listen and repeat. Use the full form of the possessive modifiers.

my friend	his book	her car	its name
our room	your class	their house	

	Full	Reduced
my	[may]	[maʸ] (mᵊ)
his	[hiz]	[iz]
her	[hᵊr]	[ᵊr]
its	[its]	[its]
our	[awᵊr]	[ar]
their	[ther]	[thᵊr]
your	[yur]	[yᵊr]

B. Listen, and fill in the possessive modifiers.

1. Where are _____my_____ keys?   2. Where's _____ car?
3. Do you have _____ keys?   4. He didn't return _____ dictionary.
5. What's _____ new address?   6. Is that _____ house?
7. I don't know _____ phone number. 8. There's _____ bank.

C. Form sentences like the example. (*Dick's a secretary. He uses a typewriter in his work.*)

1. Dick/secretary/typewriter   2. You and Tom/accountants/computer
3. Jack/carpenter/hammer   4. Heather and I/writers/dictionary
5. Joyce/artist/paintbrush   6. I/delivery person/truck

D. Listen to the reduced forms in these sentences. They are all spoken with weak stress. We use the informal spellings of *'is* for *his*, *'er* for *her*, and *yer* for *your*. These spelling forms are not appropriate for ordinary use.

1. [iz]–(his)   Is Sally 'is sister?   Yes, and Tom is 'is brother.
2. [yᵊr]–(your)   Where's yer book?   Is this yer book?
3. [ar]–(our)   Where are our tickets?   Are those our tickets?
4. [ᵊr]–(her)   What's 'er name   Is Tom 'er brother?
5. [mᵊ]–(my)   I don't have my book.   But I know my lesson.
6. [thᵊr]–(their)   That's their car.   And that's their house.
7. [its]–(its)   The dog has its water.   It's waiting for its food.

E. After a word that ends in the sound [t], *your* is pronounced [chᵊr]. If it follows a word ending in [d], it is pronounced [jᵊr].

   [t + y] = [ch]   [d + y] = [j]
   Is that your book?   Did your sister come?
   Is Pat your sister?   Don't hold your breath.
   Don't hurt your hand.   Hand your book to me.

F. Listen to these sentences. Write the possessive modifier you hear.

1. Pat's wearing _____ new suit.   2. Do you need _____ money?
3. _____ friend is coming now.   4. Kim is looking for _____ watch.
5. Please put _____ money on the table.   6. Where's _____ classroom?

G. Now listen. With each repetition of the sentence, a different possessive form is used. Write the form you hear.

Mr. Ames is talking to 1. ___our___ son. 2. _____ son. 3. _____ son.

Are these 4. _____ tickets? 5. _____ tickets? 6. _____ tickets?

We're going in 7. _____ car. 8. _____ car. 9. _____ car.

H. Name the people in the picture and tell their injuries. (*That's Tom. His leg is broken.*) Note that *his* and *her* do not lose [*h*] at the beginning of the sentence. Also tell what the various people have taken on their vacation. Use the verb *have/has*. (*Billy has his camera.*) Tell what you take on vacation or on a business trip. Ask others what they usually take.

LESSON 76
Help me help them.
Object pronouns

A. Listen and repeat the full forms of the object pronouns.

me	It helps me.	him	It helps him.
us	It helps us.	her	It helps her.
you	It helps you.	it	It helps it.
them	It helps them.		

	Full	*Reduced*	
me	[miy]	[miʸ]	
us	[əs]	[ᵊs]	
you	[yuw]	[yu]	[yᵊ]
them	[them]	[thᵊm]	[ᵊm]
him	[him]	[im]	
her	[hᵊr]	[ᵊr]	
it	[it]	[it]	

B. Listen and fill in the pronoun object.

1. Please tell   __him__ .   5. Please teach _____.

2. Please help _____.   6. Please send _____.

3. Please call _____.   7. Please take _____.

4. Please write _____.   8. Please hold _____.

C. Listen to these sentences that are spoken at normal conversational speed. All the object pronouns are spoken in reduced form with weak stress. We use the informal spellings *'im, 'er, ya,* and *'em* to represent the reduced forms of *him, her, you,* and *them.*

him	Call'im.	Tell'im.	Help'im.	her	Find'er.	Write'er.	Teach'er.
them	Buy'em.	Sell'em.	Tell'em.	it	Send it.	Forget it.	Eat it.
me	Tell me.	Help me.	Pay me.	us	Phone us.	Tell us.	Show us.
you	I'll help ya.	I'll call ya.					

Note that some phrases have the same pronunciations as single words, such as *teach'er* and *teacher, let'er* and *letter, rock it* and *rocket.*

D. After a sound that ends in the sound [d], *you* is pronounced [juw] or [jᵊ]. If it follows a word ending in [t], it is pronounced [chuw] or [chə].

We need <u>you</u>.   Who told <u>you</u>?   We heard <u>you</u>.   Who called <u>you</u>?
They want <u>you</u>.   I'll write <u>you</u>.   I won't forget <u>you</u>.   Who taught <u>you</u>?

E. Say the verb. Then say the verb and the pronoun *it*. It is very important to stress the verb.

1. Send (Send it.)   2. Sell   3. Buy   4. Stop   5. Drink   6. Eat   7. Try

F. Form sentences. Follow the model. Say the verb with loud stress and the two object pronouns with weak stress.

1. She/me (She explained it to me.)   2. She/us (She explained it to us.)
3. I/them   4. Who/him   5. We/her   6. They/them   7. He/you

LESSON   77

At the bank at noon:
Prepositional phrases

Prepositional phrases are said as a word group or unit. They usually have medium or weak stress on the preposition and loud stress on the noun. Their stress patterns form a predictable part of the rhythm of the sentences in which they occur.

A. Listen and repeat. When used with a measure or container, the word *of* is almost always pronounced in the reduced form [ᵊ]. (*cup of coffee* [kəpᵊkɔfiʸ]) Before a vowel, *of* is pronounced [ᵊv], as in box *of* oranges.

a cup of tea   a box of books   a package of gum
a line of cars   a glass of milk   a bottle of catsup
a row of desks   a bag of apples   a carton of cigarettes

B. Form noun phrases like the examples. Use the reduced form of *of*. (*a box of cookies, a big box of cookies, a big box of chocolate cookies*)

box	cup	loaf	bread	flowers	milk
bowl	dish	piece	coffee	ice cream	soup
can	glass	vase	cookies	cereal	tomatoes

C. Tell someone what you need at the grocery store or drugstore, for example, a tube of toothpaste, a bottle of milk. Use the suggestions below.

can/hair spray   can/shaving cream   bottle/lotion   package/razor blades
can/peas   carton/eggs   box/soap powder

D. Listen to and repeat the time expressions. Learn to say the phrases as units.

at two   in the morning   at six o'clock   at four in the morning

at nine   in the afternoon   in the winter   at the bank at noon

at noon   in the evening   on Tuesday   in our house at night

at night

E. Now form sentences with phrases. Tell about regular activities in your life.

(I get up at six in the morning.   Our family skis at Piney Mountain.)

F. Listen to and repeat the place expressions.

by the piano   above the sofa
on the wall   behind the door
in the desk   below the window
at the store   across the street

Now tell the location of the people and things around you.

G. A noun with a phrase modifier is spoken as a unit. First repeat the noun phrases. Then form complete sentences by using appropriate phrases from the list. (*The book on the table is for you.*)

Noun Phrases

1. The book on the table   a. is waving at us.
2. The woman at the door   b. were very competent.
3. The man in the car   c. are dirty.
4. The music on the radio   d. is a police officer.
5. The man with the gun   e. is for you.
6. The teller in the bank   f. is too loud.
7. The nurses in the hospital   g. is selling something.
8. The dishes in the sink   h. gave me the wrong change.

H. Repeat these noun phrases. Then use them as sentence subjects, completing them in any logical manner.

The man in the gray suit . . .   The book on the little table . . .
The woman with the big nose . . .   The people in the blue car . . .
The car with the flat tire . . .

Form sentences of your own, following the above pattern.

I. In conversational speech, one-word prepositions are often spoken in reduced form with weak stress.* Listen.

		Full Form		*Reduced Form*
to	[tuw]	go to the store	[tə]	go to the store
		the train to Paris		the train to Paris
for	[fɔr]	do it for fun	[fər]	do it for fun
		stay for a few days		stay for a few days
in	[in]	go in the house	[ən]	go in the house
		money in your pocket		money in your pocket
at	[æt]	stay at home	[ət]	stay at home
		come at two o'clock		come at two o'clock
from	[frəm]	come from China	[frəm]	come from China
		from here to there		from here to there
of	[əv]	a box of books	[ə] or [əv]	a box of books
		a friend of mine		a friend of mine

* This is not automatic or rigid, of course. English does not generally allow, for example, more than two or three weakly stressed syllables in a row without automatically giving medium stress to one of the words.

J. Listen. In each sentence there is one unstressed preposition spoken in reduced form. Can you hear it? Circle the preposition that you hear.

1. (at) in   2. of from   3. at up   4. to for
5. for from   6. at to   7. of in   8. in at

LESSON   78

Get up at ten
Linking of sounds

Within a phrase, sounds at word boundaries are often linked and pronounced as if they were linked into one longer word.

A. When one word ends with the same sound that the next word begins with, the result is a long sound with only one release. Repeat these phrases and then the entire sentence.

Miss Sulley	will leave	at ten.
Ten nurses	have vanished	from Maryland.
Jack Cohen	should do	more reading.
That teacher	must stop parking	in this section.

B. The second word of a linked pair may begin with a vowel. Repeat these two-word verbs, which are stressed on the second word. Then use some of them in sentences of your own.

1. get up
2. lift up
3. walk in   walked in
4. look up
5. stand up
6. rub off   rubbed off
7. give up
8. build up
9. miss out   missed out
10. sum up   summed up

Now use these noun phrases in sentences which explain their meaning.

a bald eagle   a dark alley   a rich uncle   brown ink

___

C. The police are looking for a few bad men and women. Read about two of them. Then add more to the list using some of the given words.

1. Pat Kelley is wanted for check forgery. She was last seen in White Marsh. She might look for a job as a bank teller.
2. Dave Lomax is wanted for purse snatching. He was last seen in South Bend. He might look for a job as a house painter.

Chris	Fisher	bank robbery	Big	Bend	bank teller
Dave	Jones	check forgery	Park	Cliff	bus driver
Dick	Kelley	barn burning	Steep	Marsh	brick layer
Liz	Lomax	drug dealing	South	Gate	ditch digger
Mel	Benson	purse snatching	Red	Rock	dog catcher
Pat	Taylor	safe cracking	White	Spring	house painter

D. In the following paragraph a few examples of linked words are underlined for special practice. Read the underlined linked words. Then read the paragraph.

Roscoe visited a university last week, and he got lost. First, he tried to find the library, but he went to Bliss Hall, the art building. He asked an art student from Panama, but she gave him directions to the bookstore. There he bought a campus map and found out that there were five libraries. As he walked across the campus, he noticed a student carrying a lot of books. "She must be returning them to the library," he thought. He followed her to the women's dorm. Now he was thoroughly confused. He checked the map and tried again. This time he followed the map. But several buildings looked alike. Which was the Math Pavilion? Which was Humanities? Which was the Glen Shaw Library? As darkness fell, he gave up the search and looked for his car.

LESSON 79

English is easy.
Neutral sentence stress

Whenever two or more words are used together in English, one syllable is spoken more loudly and with more force than all the others. This is called the *sentence stress* (or the *phrase stress* if only a phrase is involved). This stress is usually associated with falling intonation (⌐) or with rising intonation (⌐) if a yes-no question is being asked. Sentence stress is another element of rhythm in English speech.

How do speakers of English know where to put the phrase or sentence stress? They don't *know*; they simply *do it*. They have grown up with the language and do this without thinking and without having learned any complicated rules. In the same way, you will become more proficient in this aspect of English and in other aspects as you hear the language in class and around you. However, there are certain general observations about sentence stress that may be helpful.

We say that a sentence has *neutral* sentence stress (or neutral phrase stress) if there is no special loudness or force given to a particular word to show emphasis or contrast. Sentences with neutral sentence stress generally have the strong stress on the last noun, verb, or adjective in the sentence. We have been practicing neutral stress placement throughout this book and will continue to practice it in this lesson.

A. Listen and repeat.

Last Word

Noun	He's reading a book.	Are you buying a gift for Mary?
Verb	John's working.	Do you like to read?
Adjective	Is her car blue?	I'm not very hungry.
Adverb of Manner	He speaks English fluently.	You're doing very well.

Form sentences. Use words and phrases from columns A, B, and C (*I am reading a good book*) or from A and B (*Who fell?*).

	A	B	C	
1.	The car radio	am reading	her new address	at the door
2.	Who	is/is not	on the floor	in the hospital
3.	I/He	isn't working	easy	English
4.	English	happened	a good book	at home
5.	What	speak(s)	very hot	in China
6.	This water	fell	very well	safe

B. Listen and repeat. If a pronoun follows a final verb, the stress is on the verb.

Do you hear me?   Don't send it.   I called her.

When a noun or verb is followed by a preposition and a pronoun (*to him, in it*), the sentence stress is on the noun or verb.

Noun	Open the window for me.	Come to the movie with us.
Verb	What did he say about it?	What can we do with it?

C. Read the sentence. Then say it again and change the underlined word(s) to a pronoun. (*He's a writing a letter. He's writing it.*)

1. He's writing a letter.
2. Tell Mr. Prado about the meeting.
3. He's writing his sister.
4. Did you mail the package?
5. Open the box.
6. Did he pay a lot for the car?
7. Put some gas in the car.
8. Who called the doctor?
9. They kidnapped the boy.
10. Where did you see Mr. and Mrs. Ames?
11. Look who's dancing with Angela.
12. They handcuffed the prisoner.

D. Read the sentence. Then give advice or make a suggestion using the words in parentheses. Be sure to use a preposition and a pronoun in your sentence. Study the example. (*This lamp doesn't work. Why don't you/Maybe you'd better put a bulb in it.*)

1. This lamp doesn't work. (bulb)
2. I haven't heard from June recently. (write)
3. This radio won't work anymore. (new batteries)
4. This spot won't come out of her dress. (cleaning fluid)
5. I wonder why Tom didn't go to the party. (ask)
6. This soup is tasteless. (salt)
7. This door won't lock. (a new lock)
8. I can't get candy out of this machine. (more money)
9. I don't know where Tommy is. (look for)
10. This flashlight won't turn on. (new bulb)
11. This cut is bleeding badly. (bandage)

E. Some sentences end with a noun followed by an infinitive (called an infinitive complement). The sentence stress is on the noun: I have work to do. In such sentences the noun is the object of the infinitive. Listen and repeat.

	work to do	several bills to pay
I have	mail to answer	some telephone calls to make
	several letters to write	a few windows to wash

F. Complete the sentences with an infinitive phrase from the list.

do   correct   make   study for   read   wash today

1. I have some dirty clothes . . .
2. There's a big exam . . .
3. I have another book . . .
4. I have a few errands . . .
5. I have a suggestion . . .
6. Stan found two more mistakes . . .

LESSON 80

Burn it up.

Sentence stress (adjectives and two-word verbs)

A. Listen to and repeat these two-word verbs. The stress is on the second word.

throw away   take off   call up   write down   turn on

A noun object of a two-word verb has loud stress; a pronoun object has weak stress. Listen and repeat.

burn up   burn up the letter   burn the letter up   burn it up

try on   try on the gloves   try the gloves on   try them on

B. Tell what these people are doing. Use these two-word verbs: *put out, hang up, blow out, throw away.*

a

b

c

d

C. Answer the questions. Use a two-word verb from the list, or any other appropriate verb.

cut out	clean up	hang up	turn on
blow up	fill out	put up	look up
throw away	burn up	give away	take back

1. What do you do with papers you don't want or need any more?
2. What do you do if you can't see when you go into a room?
3. What do you do if you buy a shirt or blouse and then find it's too small when you get home?

4.   What do many people do with their old, worn-out clothes?
5.   What do you do if you spill something on the floor?
6.   What do you do when you are given an application form?
7.   What do you do if you have an umbrella and it starts to rain?
8.   What do mothers do if they find their children's clothes on the floor?
9.   What do you do if you feel a report you've written is too long?
10.   What is dynamite used for?

D.   Generally, an adjective that is the final content word in a sentence bears the sentence stress, unless, of course, strong stress has been given to some other word for emphasis or contrast. Repeat these sentences.

We were quite tíred.   Mr. White has always been very génerous.
Johnny didn't tell the trúth. That was fóolish of him.

Now read the sentences. Then read them again, substituting a pronoun for the underlined word(s).

1.   We were worried about your father. (We were worried about him.)
2.   The insurance adjuster was helpful to my parents.
3.   The music teacher was patient with Joan.
4.   Writing was never easy for Mr. Whitaker.

E.   Read the sentence. Add a second sentence. Use an appropriate adjective from the list.

1.   Mr. Longworth's taking us all to dinner. (That's very níce of him.)

2.   The Carters gave $10,000 to the hospital. (That was very génerous of them.)

3.   Bill drives too fast.

4.   The meeting is at night.

5.   You should exercise every day.

6.   Jim calls Judy all the time.

7.   Helen has been playing tennis for a long time.

8.   Thank you for changing my flat tire.

9.   Mrs. Brown left without saying good-bye.

10.   Jenny lost her wedding ring.

Adjectives:

generous of	convenient for
nice of	good for
rude of	good at
helpful of	upset about
worried about	careless of
fond of	

F. When an adjective is followed by *one* or *ones*, the adjective has strong stress.

a big tree   a big one   big office buildings   big ones

Answer with a noun phrase. Use *one* or *ones*.

1. What kind of pen do you want? (red, blue) (I want a red one./I want a blue one.)
2. What kind of books do you like? (exciting, well-written) (I like exciting ones./I like well-written ones.)
3. What kind of bed do you prefer? (soft, hard)
4. What kind of movies do you like? (romantic, humorous)
5. What kind of ties does he wear? (loud, conservative)

Continue asking questions asking about likes, dislikes, preference, and so on. A second student replies, using *one* or *ones*.

LESSON   81
He speaks English fluently.
Sentence stress (adverbs)

A final adverbial usually receives the sentence stress, especially if it adds some information that is new in the conversation. An adverbial may be a word (*soon*) or a group of words (*in a few minutes*) which indicate time, location or direction, or the manner in which something is done.

A. Listen. Then repeat the paragraph.

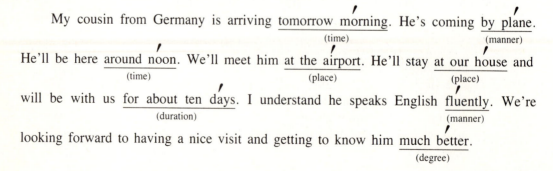

My cousin from Germany is arriving tomorrow morning. He's coming by plane.
                                            (time)   (manner)

He'll be here around noon. We'll meet him at the airport. He'll stay at our house and
          (time)   (place)   (place)

will be with us for about ten days. I understand he speaks English fluently. We're
          (duration)   (manner)

looking forward to having a nice visit and getting to know him much better.
                                                              (degree)

B. **Listen. Then repeat this paragraph. The short adverbs** *here, there, now, yet,* **and** *ago* **do not usually receive the sentence stress even when they are in final position.**

here	I arrived in Paris a few hóurs <u>ago</u>. I lóve it <u>here</u>. When I arríved, I went
there	stráight to the hotel, but my room wasn't réady <u>yet</u>. I'm not quite sure what
now	to do <u>now</u>. I think perhaps I'll go to the Lóuvre for a little while. I've réad
yet	a lot about it, of course, but I've never béen <u>there</u>.
ago	

Sometimes these short adverbs do receive the sentence stress. This is especially true after imperative verbs and when the speaker perceives a contrast of some kind. Listen and repeat.

Please sit right hére. John, you can sit over thére.

This is the lóan application. Please sign right hére.

C. **Read sentences 1 through 5. Follow each with a statement from a through e that logically follows it.** (*There's a marvelous new art exhibit at the gallery. Have you séen it yet?*)

1. There's a marvelous new art exhibit at the gallery.

2. Mary hid her ring when she went on vacation.

3. I visited San Francisco last week.

4. Here's the sales agreement for your new car.

5. Kim has asked Gay to marry him.

a. Have you ever been there?

b. She hasn't answered him yet.

c. Have you seen it yet?

d. She can't find it now.

e. You and your wife should sign right here.

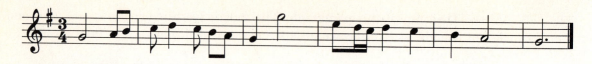

LESSON 82

His leg wasn't broken.

Contrastive stress I

Any word in a sentence may have the sentence stress. A shift in placement from normal stress position may occur for various reasons: to point out a new element in the conversation, to avoid the exact repetition of words, and very often to show special emphasis or contrast.

A. Listen and repeat.

1. Tom likes to play sóccer.   (normal stress)

    Tom likes to pláy soccer.   (not watch it or talk about it)

    Tom líkes to play soccer.   (He doesn't dislike it.)

    Tóm likes to play soccer.   (Tom, not Bob or Phil)

The basic statement and question intonation remain the same.

2.   Today is Tom's bírthday.

    Today is Tóm's birthday.

    Todáy is Tom's birthday.

3.   Do you walk to schóol?

    Do you wálk to school?

    Do yóu walk to school?

B. Now repeat these sentences.

Mrs. Todd likes to walk to wórk.   (normal stress)

Mrs. Todd likes to walk to wórk.   (But she doesn't like to walk home *from* work.)

Mrs. Todd likes to wálk to work.   (not drive or talk the bus)

Mrs. Todd líkes to walk to work.   (She doesn't dislike it.)

Mrs. Tódd likes to walk to work.   (not Mrs. Lock or Mrs. Shapiro)

Mrs. [mis⁹z] Tódd likes to walk to work.   (not her husband, Mr. Todd)

C. Listen carefully. Then mark the sentence stress. Use this mark (ˊ).

1. Where is your book?
2. What is your first name?
3. What's your last name?
4. Do you speak English?
5. Do you read it?

6. He's writing a book.
7. Did my sister call?
8. The Wilsons are giving the party.
9. I don't want to go.
10. Please give the book to me.

D. First listen to sentences 1 through 5. Then repeat them. Finally listen to the sentence and choose a second sentence (a through e) to follow it.

1. My father doesn't play tennis on Saturday.
2. My father doesn't play tennis on Saturday.
3. My father doesn't play tennis on Saturday.
4. My father doesn't play tennis on Saturday.
5. My father doesn't play tennis on Saturday.

a. He watches it.
b. My mother does.
c. Someone else's father does.
d. He plays on Sunday.
e. He plays golf.

E. Read the sentences. Explain their meaning.

1. I can't come next week.

   (I can come the week after.)

2. Ted didn't tell me.

3. She bought a red sweater.

4. His leg wasn't broken.

LESSON   83

Weaver is an English name.
Contrastive stress II

Normal stress (stress falling on the last noun, verb, adjective, or adverb) also takes the contrastive position when two content words are in opposition and come at the end of a phrase or sentence. Listen.

(adj.)   John's tall, but his brother's short.

(noun)   She's going to wear a scarf not a sweater.

(verb)   He often calls, but he never writes.

(adv.)   He isn't coming now. He's coming later.

When not in final position, the sentence stress moves to the word being contrasted or emphasized, whatever its position in the sentence.

A. Listen to the statement. Then form another sentence like the example. Use sentence stress on the contrasted noun modifier.

1. That's Helen's new silver brácelet. (gold)

   (Oh, I thought she was going to buy a góld bracelet.)

2. Here's my new French dictionary. (English)
3. Here's my new winter coat. (summer)
4. That's Tom's new red sweater. (yellow)
5. That's Laura's new wool jacket. (leather)

B. Compare two people, places, or things. Stress the adjective modifier.

1. Broadway/wide/First Street/narrow   *street*

   (Broadway is a wíde street, but First Street is a nárrow one.)

2. Weaver/English/Chang/Chinese   *name*
3. "Children"/plural/"child"/singular   *noun*
4. Norm Bolz/brilliant/H.R. Block/ordinary   *accountant*
5. South America/large/Australia/small   *continent*
6. Robert Redford/famous/Harry Ames/unknown   *actor*

C. Listen and repeat. Stress the verbs.

You can either púsh it or púll it.

You can either týpe your name or prínt it.

You can either rént your house or búy it.

You can either réad during your lunch hour or éxercise then.

Listen to each sentence. Then follow the examples and form a negative statement with the same verb and an affirmative sentence with the verb in parentheses.

1. Mary threw away her old díary. (*burn*)

   (She didn't just throw awáy her old diary. She búrned it.)

2. Bryan entered the ráce. (*win*)

   (Bryan didn't just énter the race. He wón it.)

3. Woodie Allen acts in movies. (*direct*)

4. Mr. Flaks grew the vegetables. (*can*)

5. Ken Scott designs the new dresses. (*market*)

6. Irving Berlin wrote many famous songs. (*sing*)

7. Brent Hollowell designs new houses. (*build*)

D. Use the word(s) in parentheses and form a second sentence like the model. Then read both sentences, stressing and contrasting the subjects.

1. John isn't my brother. (*Tim*)
   (John isn't my brother. Tim is.)

2. The Canadians didn't win the game. (*The Mexicans*)
   (The Canadians didn't win the game. The Mexicans did.)

3. The judge didn't decide the case. (*The jury*)

4. Southern Airways doesn't have the lowest fares. (*United Airlines*)

5. The tiger isn't the fastest jungle animal. (*The leopard*)

6. The secretary of state didn't say that. (*The president*)

7. His leg wasn't broken in the accident. (*His arm*)

8. Helen Lassiter wasn't elected president. (*Ellen Lassiter*)

9. Checking accounts don't usually pay interest. (*Savings accounts*)

LESSON 84

Do you want this pen or that one?
Contrastive stress III

A. Listen to the statement. Then form a question-word question stressing the auxiliary or form of *be*.

1. That's not John. (Who) (Who is it?)

2. I can't come tomorrow. (When) (When can you come?)

3. I can't give you the information. (Who)

4. Laura isn't going to the dance with Harold. (Who)

5. The new Thai restaurant isn't on Braddock Street. (What street)

6. The new hotel isn't finished yet. (When)

7. Mr. Jones doesn't sell insurance. (What)

8. I didn't order a hamburger. (What)

9. I didn't put the mail on your desk. (Who)

10. Tom wasn't born in New York. (Where)

B. Read these sentences stressing the contrasting demonstratives or possessive forms.

1. Do you want thís pen, or thát one?
2. Who said that — your teacher or mine?
3. Does this car or that one have more safety features?
4. Those aren't my glasses. They're yours.
5. Your car wasn't damaged. Theirs was.
6. This book wasn't very interesting, but the other one was.
7. Judy didn't tell her mother. She told my mother.

C. First read the sentences to yourself and then read them aloud. Next, listen to your teacher or the tape to see if you stressed the same words. Put a check mark if you read the sentence correctly.

Correct

1. I don't know your brother, but I know your sister.   ____
2. Your brother didn't tell me that. Your sister did.   ____
3. I can't come, but my wife will be there.   ____
4. The cat wasn't in the garage. It was on the garage.   ____
5. I didn't tell her. I told him.   ____
6. The doors aren't open. The windows are.   ____
7. The trombone isn't a stringed instrument. The piano is.   ____
8. She didn't see the thief. She heard him.   ____
9. Your book report didn't get an A. Mine did.   ____
10. He didn't say he could come. He said he couldn't come.   ____
11. A. I didn't order fish. B. What did you order, sir?   ____
12. He doesn't walk for exercise. He jogs.   ____

D. First look at the picture and the sentences. Then write a contrasting sentence to follow each of the statements. Finally, read both sentences aloud. (That's not a doctor's office. It's a dentist's office. The boy's wearing a T-shirt. He isn't wearing a sweater.)

1. That's not a doctor's office.
2. The boy's father isn't taking him to the dentist.
3. The office is on the 4th floor.
4. The number isn't 301.
5. The woman isn't knocking on the door.
6. The boy's wearing a T-shirt.
7. The woman is wearing a skirt and sweater.
8. She isn't carrying a purse under her arm.

📼   **E. Listen and repeat. Pay special attention to the contrast stresses.**

The Walters family gets its share of wrong numbers.

(1)

(Telephone rings)
Mr. Walters: Walters' residence.
   Caller 1:   Hello, may I speak to Red?
Mr. Walters: You mean Fred? Fred Walters?
   Caller 1:   No, I mean Red Walters.
                 Say, is this 8691?
Mr. Walters: No, this is 7691.
   Caller 1:   Oh, I'm sorry.

(2)

(Telephone rings)
Mrs. Walters: Hello.
    Caller 2:   Hello, do I have the Carter residence?
Mrs. Walters: No, this is the Walters' residence.
                  You must have the wrong number. This is 228-7691.
    Caller 2:   Oh, yes. That's my mistake.
                  I was trying to dial 227-7671. Excuse me.
Mrs. Walters: That's quite all right.

📼   **F. Read these paragraphs. How many examples of contrast stress can you find? Then listen to the tape or your teacher and read the paragraphs again.**

Exercising for Fun and Health

We all know the value of exercise, but does everyone do it? We should—and not one day a week, but at least three days a week. And not for ten minutes each time, but for at least thirty minutes. And steady exercise is much better than doing it in bits and pieces. It's also a good idea to do different activities on different days. Swim one day, ride a bike another. Walk one time, jog the next time.

And what about walking? It's the best exercise of all. However, a fast walk is better than a slow one, but any walk is better than no walk. On sunny days you can enjoy a walk in the fresh air, and on rainy days you can do what a lot of people are doing—walk in a mall! But is walking as good as jogging or running? Experts say it is. Jogging and running sometimes cause injury to the knee; walking seldom causes difficulty.

 **UNIT SEVEN**

Final Practice and Review

In this pronunciation course you have practiced the English sounds and the intonation and rhythm of simple sentences. Now here's your chance to review many of the things you learned. Finally, you can see how you rate on the twenty-item check-up quiz.

A. Read these conversational exchanges. Decide how you are going to say them. Then take parts on tape or with a partner. Be prepared to take either part.

1. A. Where's Joe?

   B. I don't know. I haven't seen him.

2. A. Is that your blue car over there?

   B. No. Mine's the one next to it. The white one.

3. A. Where's your brother?

   B. I think he's at the office. Why?

4. A. Do you like these gloves?

   B. Yes. They're very nice.

   A. Well, try them on.

   B. Hmm. Yes, they're fine. How much are they?

   A. $7.95.

   B. Okay. I'll take them.

5. A. I didn't order the turkey.

   B. What did you order?

6. A. I can't come next Monday.

   B. Well, when can you come?

7. A. Is your house the second house or the third house from the corner?

   B. It's the third house.

8. A. Mr. Paine, I want you to meet Mr. Waters.

   B. I'm glad to know you, Mr. Waters.

   C. I'm glad to meet you, sir.

9. A. Are you going to Kim's party?

   B. No, I can't. I have some work to do.

10. A. Hey, Sal! Wait up!

    B. Hi! What's up?

    A. Nothing. Let's stop at Cory's on the way home.

11. A. May I come in?

    B. Yes, please do. Take your coat off and have a seat.

B. Tell the story of the pictures in your own words. Use some of these words.

cold	gold	thief	flashlight	trip on
fan	van	cord	young woman	tie up
safe	save	cap	arrest	take off
rope	robe	head	sweater	put on
hat	had	gun	police	pick up

Listen to the questions. Answer them.

1. What did the (man/men) do?
2. Who had the (rope/robe)?
3. Where was the (fan/van?)
4. Who (laughed/left)? When? Why?
5. Where was the young woman's (cab/cap)?

C. Words in these sentences are spoken in reduced form. Listen and put a check in front of the form you hear. (*Use a pencil so you can erase your answers and do the practice again*.)

1. Where's { _____ her / _____ your } car?

2. { _____ Did you / _____ Did she } tell him?

3. I can't see { _____ him / _____ them } now.

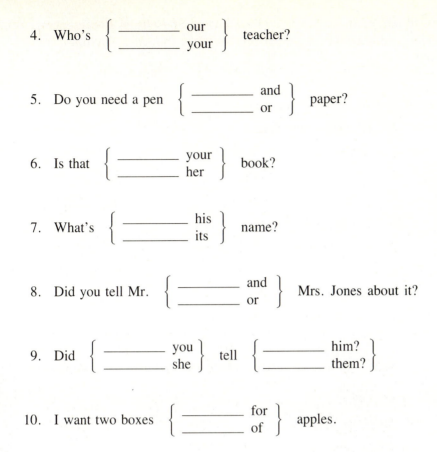

4. Who's { _____ our / _____ your } teacher?

5. Do you need a pen { _____ and / _____ or } paper?

6. Is that { _____ your / _____ her } book?

7. What's { _____ his / _____ its } name?

8. Did you tell Mr. { _____ and / _____ or } Mrs. Jones about it?

9. Did { _____ you / _____ she } tell { _____ him? / _____ them? }

10. I want two boxes { _____ for / _____ of } apples.

Now listen to the dialogs two or three times. Then in the blanks write the questions or sentences you hear. Write the full forms of the pronouns.

1. A. I saw Jim yesterday.
   B. Oh? _____
   A. Same thing. He's still in advertising.
   A. _____
   B. He's still with Hatfield's.

2. A. I bought Helen a birthday present today.
   B. _____
   A. Next week.
   B. _____
   A. A little camera.

3. A. Hey! Look at my new red sock!
   B. Oh great! _____
   A. I didn't.
   _____

4. A. _____
   B. No. I'm not hungry yet.
   C. Well, I am.
   _____

D. **Listen to the rhythm of these two model sentences. Then listen to sentences 1 through 10 and check the column whose model sentence has the same rhythm.**

The baby cries a lot.   They did not come on time.

_____	1. We won't arrive at noon.	_____
_____	2. He enjoyed the parade.	_____
_____	3. A woman got there first.	_____
_____	4. What a day for a walk!	_____
_____	5. Umbrellas cost too much.	_____
_____	6. The lion gets his share.	_____
_____	7. It's a shame you can't stay.	_____
_____	8. That's my car over there.	_____
_____	9. When will Brown call New York?	_____
_____	10. Who laughed at Smith's mistake?	_____

Listen to and repeat these well-known jingles. Mark the syllables with loud stress.

1. *Two, four, six, eight,*

   Who do we appreciate?

2. *Double, double, toil and trouble*

   Fire burn and cauldron bubble.

3. *Run, run as fast as you can;*

   You can't catch me, I'm the gingerbread man.

4. *How much wood would a woodchuck chuck,*

   If a woodchuck would chuck wood?

E. **Listen to these two poems. Mark the strong stresses on the last lines of each.**

1.   *At the Shore*

   Nothing goes on at the shore today;
   No birds fly, no dolphins play.
   Nothing goes on at the shore, and yet
   I am suddenly dripping wet.

   By Harriet Sheeler

2.   *Inland*

Back of the sea on the waterway
Where the heron stands and the swallows play,
Surely now is the nicest time of day
When the sun sets.
Then the fog rolls in and things disappear
Until there's nothing that's really near—
Just the fog, just the fog, just the fog.

By Harriet Sheeler

Listen to these poems and mark the strong stresses.

3.   *A Wise Old Owl*

A wise old owl lived in the oak.
The more he saw, the less he spoke.
The less he spoke, the more he heard.
Why aren't we all like that wise old bird?

4.   *A Bird Came*
              Down the Walk

A bird came down the walk:*
He did not know I saw;
He bit an angleworm in halves
And ate the fellow, raw.*

* walk = path   raw = uncooked

By Emily Dickinson

5.   *Annabel Lee*

It was many and many a year ago,
*   In a kingdom by the sea,*
That a maiden there lived whom you may know
*   By the name of Annabel Lee;—*
And this maiden she lived with no other thought
*   Than to love and be loved by me.*

By Edgar Allan Poe

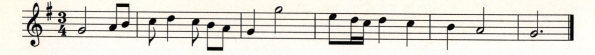

Self Check up

Here's your opportunity to test your ability to hear and respond to the sounds and rhythms of English. Listen carefully and mark your answers.

A. Which do you hear? Circle a or b.

1. Bring that _____ over here please.

   a. fan

   b. van

2. I didn't catch the _____ near here.

   a. bass

   b. bus

3. How fast can you _____ these eggs?

   a. shell

   b. sell

4. What happened to the _____ of this shirt?

   a. color

   b. collar

5. _____ today, gone tomorrow.

   a. Here

   b. Hair

6. You have to order the fish _____ the soup.

   a. and

   b. or

7. When did _____ enter the country?

   a. we

   b. he

8. At only _____ dollars this is a bargain.

   a. 16

   b. 60

9. How much is _____?

   a. $28 - (2 \times 6)$

   b. $(28 - 2) \times 6$

10. a. Judge Évans decided the Samson vs. Goliath´ case.

    b. Judge Évans´ decided the Samson vs. Goliath case.

B. Listen to the question. How do you answer? Circle a or b.

11. a. The 42 bus.

    b. A poem.

12. a. It was too expensive.

    b. He liked it there.

13. a. Yes, it's over $50,000.

    b. Yes, it's almost an acre.

14. a. Sure, can't you open it?

    b. Sure, can't you move it?

15. a. He made a big mistake.

    b. He won the game for them.

16. a. That big one over there.

    b. Those sitting on the table.

17. a. $30.00.

    b. $100.00

18. a. He spends hours at his homework.

    b. She asks questions in class.

19. a. Later this afternoon.

    b. At 4:30.

20. a. Jím´ already cleaned it.

    b. Jim already cléaned´ it.

What is your total number of correct answers? ☐

Teacher Notes and Answer Key

UNIT One   An Overview of English Pronunciation

The overview section is intended to be an introduction to the essential components of the English sound system. Several research studies have shown that students profit from listening at length to a new language before they attempt to use the language themselves. It is not essential that they know all the words in the section, although it is likely that they will be acquainted with most of the elementary vocabulary and simple sentence structures. Listening to this section will introduce the student to many of the basic building blocks of the English language. Repeated listening to this section before beginning intensive and specialized practice will give the student an introduction to and a feel for the language—how everything works together. It is essential that students understand and be able to respond to the directions given on tape or by the teacher in this introductory section. The following directions are used:

> *Listen. Listen carefully. Listen to . . . the sentences . . . to the words and sentences . . . to this sound . . . to these two sounds . . . to the word pairs . . . to the dialog . . . to the reading. Look at the picture. Also, follow the directions in your book.*

This last direction is used with exercises where the student is asked to participate in discrimination exercises. You will need to explain and demonstrate exactly what the student is expected to do with these listening exercises.

The overview section is recorded on tape with just enough hesitation between items to allow the students to absorb the material and to voice it to themselves if they choose to do so.

This overview section can also be used for additional classroom practice or used as a diagnostic tool with more advanced students. With such students, you may also wish to practice a section or sections and then turn to different lessons in the book for more in-depth practice.

When doing the lessons of the text proper, the students will benefit from going back to the overview tape from time to time to look again at all the components of the sound system and to recognize how the particular point they are practicing fits into the whole picture.

Words **A.** We recognize three levels of tone—high, middle, low. This falling tone from high to low is often used at the end of a phrase or sentence. In this section, each word constitutes a phrase by itself.

B. Stressing the correct syllable of a word is part of the correct pronunciation of a word, along with saying the vowels and consonants correctly.

C. 2. da dá   8. dá da da   **D.** 2. dá da da   7. da dá

3. dá da   9. dá da da   3. dá da   8. dá da da

4. dá da   10. da dá da   4. da dá da   9. da dá

5. da dá   11. dá da da   5. da dá   10. da dá da

6. dá da   12. da dá da   6. da da dá   11. da da dá

12. da dá da

F. The student must learn to recognize weak-stressed syllables, which are short and weak and therefore hard to hear as syllables.

F. 2. (2) writing   **H.** 2. Fóster   **I.** 2. re·péat   **K.** 2. Robérta

3. (2) order   3. Diáne   3. án·swer   3. Aníta

4. (2) English   4. Róbert   4. ó·pen   4. Márian

5. (1) play   5. Jeróme   5. fín·ish   5. Lucínda

6. (3) department   6. Eláine   6. pro·nóunce   6. Cláudia

7. (1) friend   8. Perú   7. ex·pláin

8. (2) playing   9. Chína   8. tráv·el

9. (3) mechanic   10. Éngland

10. (3) December   11. Brazíl

11. (3) enjoying   12. Égypt

12. (2) New York

Phrases and Sentences **A.** The phrase and sentence stress are marked thus: [✓]. This is the loudest or dominant stress in the phrase or sentence.

Stress practice in this book will concentrate on the phrase or sentence stress. (Another note regarding the stress markings and phrase stress is found in Unit 2, Lesson 4.) A *phrase* in grammatical terms is a group of words without a subject and verb. A *sentence* is a group of words that presents a topic (the subject) and says something about that topic (the predicate).

C. 2. clássroom   **H.** 1. mán   5. Ánn

3. guitár   2. Mr. Jóhnson   6. désk

4. Itálian   3. dó   7. dóing

5. Tháiland   4. Énglish   8. létter

6. óffice

I, L. In future lessons, the stress marks and intonation arrows are used interchangeably. Use of the stress marks focuses attention on stress; the arrows remind the student of intonation patterns, particularly the rising or falling tone at the end of a sentence.

L. 1. Spanish   **N.** 1. ↘ Mary is sleeping.   **O.** 1. síster

2. speak it   2. ↗ Was Mary writing letters?   2. garáge

3. desk   3. ↘ What is her name?   3. meet yóu

4. letters   4. ↘ Her name is Anne.   4. rúnway

5. New York   5. ↗ Is the ball on the chair?

6. know her   6. ↘ The baby is on the floor.

7. student   7. ↗ Did you hear the question?

8. hear me   8. ↗ Are the children in school?

Vowels The words in the boxes have been chosen for their variety of sounds (allophones) and for the different spellings that the phoneme may have. Explain to the students that on tape all of the words in the boxes are read from left to right—the two on the left, and then the two on the right. Thus the sound [ae] is read this way: [ae], [ae], man, that, thank, class. The words are then followed by the illustrative phrases or sentences: That man. Thank you.

C. Tell the students that the series of sentences are read consecutively, <u>without</u> saying the numbers.

D. Explain to the students that the sounds are introduced first on tape, and then the word pairs are rendered. For example: [ey], [ey], they, radio, eight, name, and then the word pairs [e] vs. [ey]: let–late, tell–tale. After this the sentences are read.

Consonants With few exceptions, the consonants are represented by common spellings. The students need only to recognize the few that are different; they do not need to use the symbols themselves. (Refer to

Unit 5 for more information about consonants.) Voiceless consonants symbols are printed in light face type, and voiced consonants and all vowels are in bold.

D. The tape for Part D is slightly different. First the sound [p] is introduced; next the contrasting phoneme [b]. Then the contrasting pairs are read. The same procedure is followed for the phonemes [t] and [d], and finally [k] and [g].

Rhythm Note that the *word stress pattern* of the content word (noun, verb, adjective, adverb) does not change when the word appears in a phrase or sentence. One syllable, however, does receive a louder stress call at the phrase or sentence stress.

2. dóc·tor   6. líves . . . a·párt·ment   11. pláne . . . Lón·don . . . lánd·ing

3. fríend   7. um·brél·la bró·ken   12. bá·by . . . a·sléep . . . béd

4. léav·ing   8. háir . . . lóng   13. thrów·ing . . . báll . . . fríend

          9. báll . . . cháir   14. lét·ter . . . tá·ble . . . yóu

The Sound of English **A.** The student will hear conversations against the sounds of background noise: street and playground sounds, the blowing of wind and rain, a running train, and dishes rattling as the waiter brings in the meal. The student should match the pictures in terms of the background noises he hears.

A. 1-*b.* (Conversations)

Joe: Run! Faster! We're getting soaked.
Jan: The drugstore over there is open. Go that way.
Joe: Watch out for that curb!
Jan: O.K. I see it. Don't wait for me. Hurry! Oh, that wind is *so* strong!
Joe: Whew: Here we are.
Jan: Gosh. That storm sure came up in a hurry.

2-*c*

Mr. Larsen: What kind of business are you in, Ms. Toron?
Ms. Toron: I work for a publishing company in New Jersey. I'm an editor.
Mr. Larsen: That sounds like an interesting job. An important one, too.
Ms. Toron: And you, Mr. Larsen? Said you were a buyer?
Mr. Larsen: I buy clothing for the Fortuna Department Stores in Denver.
Ms. Toron: Oh! Well, maybe you can give me some advice?
Mr. Larsen: Sure, if I can. Oh, look over there!
Ms. Toron: Yes. Isn't that interesting. I must say I do enjoy traveling this way for a change.

3-*a*

Carol: What's the name of the restaurant where we're going?
Brian: Papillon.
Carol: I like Italian food.
Brian: No, it's French.
Carol: Oh, yes, of course. Now how many are coming to lunch?
Brian: Just two—Jim Waters—he's the contract officer, and Jane Chu, she's a vice-president.
Carol: Well, let's hope they're interested in our proposal. We need that contract.
Brian: I'll say we do. Oh, here we are.

B. 1. Our next conference will be held in New York.
     2. He went to New York twice last year.
     3. In New York you always get a feeling of excitement.
     4. The weather in London isn't always like this.
     5. She went to London to visit the queen.
     6. Grace left London in October and got to China in June.
     7. Our plane landed at the airport in Toronto.
     8. Toronto is Canada's largest city, but it isn't the capital.

9. Niagara Falls is just a short distance from downtown Toronto.
10. The president stayed in Washington for the whole summer.
11. I can't remember when Washington was built.
12. Baltimore's a port city, but Washington isn't.

C. 1. Yes There's a lot to see in New York.
   2. No   How shall we celebrate the new year?
   3. No   It doesn't cost much to call Lisbon on weekends.
   4. Yes The city of London has changed a lot in 200 years.
   5. Yes They're having a hard winter in Toronto this year.
   6. No   Like most big cities, Boston has a subway.

D. 1. Where there's smoke, there's fire.
   2. Many hands make light work.
   3. Drive safely. The life you save may be your own.
   4. It never rains but it pours.
   5. Everybody talks about the weather, but nobody does anything about it.
   6. Fourscore and seven years ago, our fathers brought forth on this continent a new nation.

E. 1. F
   2. N
   3. N
   4. F
   5. N
   6. F

F. a-*2 people* (Conversation)

George: Are you free for lunch, Al?
   Tom: I'm planning to eat at my desk this noon, George. I've got a lot of work to catch up on.
George: Joan Corbett from Electronic Futures is coming over.
   Tom: Is that the new account you were talking about?
George: Well, not yet, but we're hoping to get it. It would be good for you to meet her.
   Tom: Yeah, I agree. I'm join you. What time?
George: Oh, that's great. One o'clock — in my office.

b-*3 people* (Conversation)

 Mary: Is Tom still working so hard?
Nancy: Yes, and I'm beginning to get worried about him.
 Mary: Alan and I are planning a trip to Mexico in April. Why don't you and Tom go along with us?
Nancy: Sounds great to me, but I don't know. Fred, you and Eleanor lived there, didn't you?
 Fred: Yes — we were in Mexico for six years. Eleanor was assigned there. We loved it and know you would.
 Mary: Yes, Fred's the one who interested us in going. Alan and I are learning a little Spanish. Why don't you talk to Tom?
Nancy: You know, I think I will. We promised we'd take a good vacation this year.

c-*2 people*

Joyce: I can't believe this. I've looked everywhere for my purse. Where could it be? Billy, have you seen my purse anywhere?
Billy: Huh-uh.
Joyce: Oh, thank goodness. Here it is. Now if your father calls, tell him I'll be back at four o'clock, will you?
Billy: Uh-huh.
Joyce: Now, don't forget to clean up your room, and cut the lawn. And don't forget your homework.
Billy: Aw, Mom.
Joyce: Bye, sweetheart.
Billy: Bye.

UNIT Two   Basic Stress, Rhythm and Intonation

Lessons 1–12 These lessons give rhythm practice with parts of sentences—noun phrases as subjects and objects—and with prepositional phrases. Mastery of these separate entities will help the student with the overall rhythm of his speech.

Lesson 1 **B.** 1. S pencil, paper
2. D June, July
3. S speaker, dirty
4. D China, Brazil
5. D study, explain
6. S asking, answer

C. 1. again
2. forget
3. paper
4. window
5. repeat
6. answer
7. English
8. above

D. 2. prac·tice
3. mu·sic
4. win·dow
5. an·swer
6. Bra·zil
7. bal·loon
8. Pe·ru
9. gui·tar

Lesson 2 **B.** 1. D elephant, banana
2. S officer, president
3. S eraser, tomorrow
4. D bicycle, apartment
5. D ordering, enjoying
6. S Roberta, Lucinda

C. 1. sentences
2. Atlantic
3. medical
4. president
5. piano
6. tobacco

D. eleven

F. 1. satisfy 5. architect
2. telephone 6. Lebanese
3. Japanese 7. diplomat
4. educate 8. substitute

G. 1. Chev·ro·let 2. rep·re·sent 3. un·der·stand
4. pho·to·graph 5. hol·i·day 6. cig·a·rette

Lesson 3 **C.** 2. In/At the post office.
3. A swimming suit.
4. (Some) eyeglasses.
5. In/At the doctor's office.
6. In/At the bookstore.

E. blackboard, classroom, English teacher, homework, notebook, textbook, tape recorder

F. airport ticket agent airline airplanes plane tickets air travel airline pilot

G. 2. drinking water
3. wrapping paper
4. raincoat
5. salesperson

H. 2. a person who fights fires
3. a machine used for making ice
4. a car that runs on cables
5. a mechanic who works on autos
6. a ball used in bowling
7. a knife used for cutting and spreading butter
8. a professor who teaches history
9. a horse that races
10. a race run by horses
11. a map that shows roads

Lesson 4 This section introduces the phrase or sentence stress. We use a four-stress system. Three of them are used in words: astronaut. In any phrase or sentence one syllable is stressed more loudly than the others, and this syllable is given the phrase or sentence stress (the fourth stress: The ˚ˊastronaut ˚˙was ˚ˊready˚).

C. 1. a. ˊteacher   b. Énglish teacher

2. a. ˊoffice   b. ˊbookkeeper

3. a. ˊSpanish   b. Madrˊid

4. a. ˊpens   b. cˊents

5. a. ˊLondon   b. tomorˊrow

6. a. ˊairline pilot   b. Amˊerica now

Lessons 5 and 6   The stress and intonation systems in English are separate and distinct systems. However, there is a high degree of concurrence between the sentence stress and the high tone of the intonation pattern. Thus, we can assign either an intonation arrow or a stress mark to the loudest stress of a sentence to indicate both stress and intonation phenomena.

D. 2. ˊquestion   7. ˊname?   **F.** 2. ⌐note·book.

3. ˊsix   8. ˊlive?   3. ⌐trav·el a·gent.

4. ˊsister   9. ˊdo?   4. ⌐ad·dress.

5. ˊwork   10. ˊstudent.   5. ⌐pi·lot.

6. ˊhospital   11. ˊaccountant.   6. ⌐tel·e·phone num·ber

12. ˊairline pilot

Lesson 6   **C.** 2. ⌣Italian   **D.** 2. Does he speak French?

3. ⌣teacher   3. Is she thirsty?

4. ⌣America   4. Does she like fruit?

5. ⌣lawyer   5. Are they watching TV?

6. ⌣tennis   6. Do they live in New York?

7. ⌣class   7. Are we late?

8. ⌣car   8. Does he swim?

9. Is she a professor?

10. Does she drink coffee?

Lesson 8   **C.** 1. ˊtable   2. Énglish   3. ˊbaby   4. ˊeasy language   5. ˊlunch   6. cˊoats

D, E.   Understanding these two sections will give the student an insight into the basic elements of the stress-timed rhythm of English.

As a very general rule, the content words (as exemplified in Part D retain their strong word stress, while grammar or function words have reduced stress—either medium or weak.

F. 1. is, a   5. is
2. is, my   6. and, are
3. is, a   7. She, in, an
4. Is, he, a   8. He, the, on, the

Lesson 9   An understanding of the general principles outlined in Lesson 8 makes possible the practice in Lesson 9: the patterned sentences and the poetry lines. The weak stresses are crowded in between the content words which have strong stresses. To speakers of a language such as Spanish, with its staccato-type rhythm—each syllable with its full vowel pronounced equally, and a strong stress at the end of the utterance—the English-type rhythm is completely alien. It takes some practice to render sentences intelligibly or at least without a pronounced Spanish accent.

    E. Poetry rhythm exhibits one of the clearest and most-often exaggerated examples of English rhythm. Poetry is subject to different interpretations, and thus different rhythmic patterns. Do not be surprised or disturbed if your patterning differs from the markings of the poems in the text, here and elsewhere.

UNIT Three   Vowels

Vowel lessons are arranged so that individual vowel sounds are practiced first, and then the contrast between them (e.g.: (1) [i], (2) [iy], (3) [i] vs. [iy]. We start with front vowels because students can easily see the tongue position.

Note that in *Sounds and Rhythm* we indicate the distinctive sounds of English (the phonemes) in brackets: [ ]. These have sound variations (allophones) in different environments, which we do not mark but do sometimes mention in the Teacher Notes. For example, the sound [p] has at leaset three variations: it is produced with an accompanying puff of air when at the beginning of a stressed syllable (as in *pin*), it has no accompanying puff of air after the sound [s] (as in *spin*), and at the end of a word or phrase it may be produced without releasing the lip closure (as in *cup*).

Lesson 13 **A, B, C** In many languages the five vowel sounds are unglided or, "pure." In English all but [a] have an off-glide—a movement from one vowel sound to another. For example, in a word such as "say," the vowel [e] moves to a higher front position with lips spreading to the sound [i], giving [ey]. In a word such as "toe," the vowel [o] moves to a higher back with a tighter lip-rounding to give [ow]. Point out these differences to the students and give some concentrated practice with them. You can locate all the English vowel sounds on the facial diagram in "C." Also refer to the facial diagram whenever doing subsequent lessons.

    D. The three vowels on the bottom row are called dipthongs because they begin with a low vowel and end with a high off-glide.

    E. Phrases 1–8 each contain two examples of the same vowel sound. Ask students to tell you what they are.

Lesson 14 The length of vowels is extremely important for efficient communication in English because vowels help to distinguish between succeeding voiced and voiceless consonants. Vowel length becomes especially important when preventing confusion between two similar-sounding words.

    A. In class, explain and practice each new type of exercise. Exercises of this type (*Listen to pairs of words and circle the one that has the shorter vowel*) are read twice on tape, and time is allowed for the student to circle the appropriate number. Example: bed-bet/bed-bet (pause) 1 2 .

    A. 4. bed bet   5. foot food   6. sad sat   7. coat code   8. bang bank

    B. Vowels in stressed syllables are longer. A word ending in a stressed vowel has the longest vowel sound of all. In these pairs—seed-sea and cave-Kay—the words *see* and *Kay* have the longer vowel.

    C. 2. It's a fat rat.   3. It's a blue shoe.
          4. It's a long song.   5. It's a gray day.
          6. It's a big pig.   6. It's good wood.
          8. It's nice ice.

Lesson 15 **A.** 1. Tom   2. clock   3. back   4. lock
              5. sing   6. box   7. look   8. cut
              9. cot   10. John

B. In exercises in which words are underlined, the tape voices the underlined words separately, and then gives the phrase or sentence in which they occur. You may wish to extend practice in class following this procedure.

Lesson 16 **A.** 1. eyes 2. rice 3. race 4. tape
5. type 6. heat 7. hate 8. height
9. mine 10. seen

Lesson 17 The sound [i] (sit) is not just a shorter version of [iy] (seat) (See Lessons 18 and 19). The tongue is lower and muscles are more relaxed. There is no off-glide.

A. 1. his 6. sting **G.** 1. vines, vineyard
2. sit 7. pill 2. five, fifth
3. seat 8. peel 3. dinner, dining
4. fish 9. same 4. children, child
5. fight 10. wit 5. wise, wisdom

Lesson 18 **A.** 1. please **C.** 2. Please see me in three weeks.
2. list 3. He's leaving in the evening.
3. least 4. Eva likes cream in her tea.
4. sheep 5. She's never seen these machines.
5. time 6. Teenagers eat a lot of pizza.
6. slip
7. sea
8. sign
9. sleep
10. live

Lesson 19 As you know, the contrasting sounds [i] and [iy] require considerable practice for acceptable pronunciation and comprehension. You will undoubtedly need to give more practice than is given in this short lesson. In class, and in succeeding lessons, you can continue to focus on these contrasting phonemes.

A. 1. D slip, sleep 7. [iy] weak
2. S hit, hit 8. [i] kick
3. S beat, beat 9. [i] six
4. D hit, heat 10. [iy] leave
5. S did, did 11. [i] lived
6. D fit, feet 12. [i] bring

C. As a variant, have students read the questions.
1. *a*–sheep 2. *a*–live 3. *a*–fill 4. *b*–heat

Lesson 20 **A.** Make sure students know how to do the exercise in this section. You can easily extend it for more class practice. As a variation and to concentrate on student pronunciation, have a student say a word and his or her classmate or partner determine whether the sound produced has the vowel sound [e].

A. 1. egg 6. leave
2. late 7. get
3. kind 8. gate
4. let 9. friend
5. said 10. heavy

E. 1. I felt well. 8. He fed his pet.
2. He met a friend. 9. He said hello.
3. I went by jet. 10. It held ten pens.
4. She read a letter. 11. He meant farewell.
5. I left at eleven. 12. She bled a lot.
6. She fell on the steps. 13. She kept it in the second drawer.
7. I slept in the bed. 14. He led them to a French restaurant.
15. He crept in the bedroom.

Lesson 21 **A.** 1. said   6. main
2. wait   7. gave
3. name   8. let
4. noun   9. plate
5. line   10. strange

Lesson 22 **A.** 1. S   tell   tell   7. [e]   let   **D.** 1. *b*–sell
2. S   raid   raid   8. [ey]   pay   2. *b*–test
3. D   tell   tale   9. [e]   pen   3. *a*–pain
4. S   red   red   10. [ey]   late   4. *a*–chess
5. D   wed   wade   11. [ey]   ache
6. D   get   gate   12. [e]   egg

Lesson 23 **A.** 1. lid   **C.** (Example answers)
2. pens   1. in a minute
3. miss   2. a nice red pen
4. spill   3. the rest of the men
           4. Give me a drink.

Lesson 24 **A.** 1. can   6. hat
2. caught   7. back
3. class   8. rang
4. hot   9. laugh
5. met

B. Some speakers pronounce the sound [ae] differently in certain words. These speakers use the regular low tongue position for [ae] in the words *hat, cat, back, rang, baffle* and the like. They use a raised form of [ae] in words like *bad, cab, man, half, cash,* making such words sound quite different. Students may notice different-sounding vowels in the [ae] words of some English speakers. These dialect pronunciations are an indication of the speaker's native region. American English has no one, universal accepted standard pronunciation, and several varieties (but not all varieties) are acceptable. Students will be accustomed to hearing some of the variations in the pronunciation of [ae] and other vowel sounds.

Lesson 25 **A.** 1. [ae] [a]   hat   hot
2. [a] [a]   not   not
3. [ae] [a]   add   odd
4. [ae] [a]   can   cot
5. [ae] [a]   sad   John
6. [ae] [ae]   flag   sat

D. You may wish to point out that while *can't* uses the full vowel [ae], the affirmative *can* (when used before a verb) is usually pronounced with the reduced vowel [ə]: I can go / ay kən gow/.

F. 1. [e]   Ted   **G.** 1. men   **I.** 1. *a*–tap   **J.** 1. Spanish, Spain; 2. shade, shadows;
2. [ae]   Jan   2. pat   2. *a*–pain   3. bathe, bath;   4. sane, sanity
3. [e]   Brett   3. guess   3. *a*–rake
4. [ae]   Sally   4. laughed
5. [e]   Ben
6. [e]   Ned
7. [ae]   Pam
8. [ae]   Sam

Lesson 26 **A, B.** The words of each group are placed in a position that suggests the tongue position—front or back, high or low.

       A. 1. 1. bit   2. 1. lid   3. 1. Dane
             2. bat   2. let   2. dean
             3. beat   3. laid   3. den
             4. bait   4. lead   4. Dan
             5. bet   5. lad   5. din

B. 1. She came in at ten.
2. Ted hates his Greek class.
3. Each place has six beds.
4. Ann still bakes sweet bread.

C. Bingo. This particular exercise is easily expanded and may be used with other vowel and consonant sections. Make your own cards, focusing on one or two particular vowels and consonants, to distribute in class. You may also have a student call out the words.

1. need	11. man
2. name	12. ten
3. seat	13. best
4. fat	14. main
5. feel	15. be
6. pig	16. bill
7. mail	17. let
8. hand	18. red
9. bake	19. cave
10. fit	20. match

D. This tongue twister is given here for practice with the vowels [i], [e], [ae] and [ə]. It also features the medial flapped [t]. Students might be asked to explain why the butter is bitter (it's sour or rancid, etc.) or what batter is and what it's used for. People usually recite this poem without noticing that the last line is somewhat illogical; that is, since Betty never used the bitter butter, her batter is never bitter.

Lesson 27 A.
1. long   6. coffee
2. odd   7. boat
3. off   8. draw
4. small   9. clock
5. book   10. wrong

Lesson 28 Students whose native language employs only a pure or simple vowel [o] need practice in producing the glide that goes from approximately [o] to [u].

A.
1. lock   6. phoning
2. boat   7. rang
3. home   8. walking
4. call   9. woke
5. coat   10. ago

Lesson 29 A.
1. S caught, caught	7. [ɔ] soft	**F.** 1. a–call
2. D caught, coat	8. [ow] slow	2. a–loan
3. D sew, saw	9. [ɔ] law	3. a–cost
4. S called, called	10. [ow] low	4. b–bald
5. D bowl, ball	11. [ow] home	
6. D cold, called	12. [ɔ] small	

Lesson 30 A.
1. [ɔ] ball
2. [a] doctor
3. [ɔ] talking
4. [ɔ] ought
5. [a] bottle

Lesson 31 The vowel [ə], called schwa, is difficult and new for almost all students. Considerable practice in distinguishing [ə] (nut) from [a] (not) (See Lesson 32) will be needed throughout your pronunciation work with students. [ə] is not just a shortened form of [a]; the tongue and jaw are raised.

A.
1. luck   6. truck
2. money   7. not
3. box   8. nut
4. coming   9. enough
5. another 10. lock

D. Number 8: Note that "who" is used here because of our focus on the spoken language. In writing, "whom" would undoubtedly be used.

Lesson 32 **A.** 1. [a] [a] lock lock   4. [ə] [a] much not
                      2. [ə] [a] fund fond   5. [ə] [a] cut cot
                      3. [ə] [ə] touch run   6. [ə] [ə] done much

C. The things under the hut are watch, glove, money. Why are they there? Did someone lose them? Did someone steal them and hide them there?

D. 1. *a*–dock   **F.** 1. *b*–rag
       2. *b*–rubber   2. *a*–cup
       3. *b*–knots   3. *a*–ankle
       4. *a*–color   4. *b*–track

Lesson 33 **A.** 1. look   6. room
                      2. boot   7. wouldn't
                      3. should   8. borrow
                      4. push   9. lucky
                      5. cold   10. cooking

Lesson 34 **A.** 1. blow   6. down
                      2. blue   7. threw
                      3. soon   8. throw
                      4. gone   9. moonlight
                      5. school   10. choosing

Lesson 35 Not many languages have this contrast. Work in additional practice as you go along and opportunities arise during the course.

A. 1. S look   look   7. [uw] spoon   **B.** 1. [uw]
       2. D pull   pool   8. [u] cook   2. [uw]
       3. D look   Luke   9. [uw] who   3. [u]
       4. S stood   stood   10. [u] woman   4. [uw]
       5. D fool   full   11. [u] soot
       6. D should shoed   12. [uw] doing

Lesson 36 **A.** 1. lock   **2.** 1. cod   **3.** 1. Paul   **B.** 1. Bob just bought two old books.
                      2. Luke   2. code   2. pole   2. Tom should walk home from school.
                      3. look   3. cooed   3. pool   3. Joe lost one good blue sock.
                      4. luck   4. could   4. pull
                                       5. cawed
                                       6. cud

C. 1. should, boardwalk   **D.** Bingo Words
       2. John's, clothes, laundry   1. food   11. loose
       3. bottom, full, socks   2. bus   12. most
                                            3. dawn   13. walk
                                            4. rose   14. look
                                            5. fun   15. soon
                                            6. bush   16. should
                                            7. wood   17. full
                                            8. boat   18. hope
                                            9. cause   19. coat
                                           10. blood   20. bone

Lesson 39 **B.** 1. I want rye bread without those raw seeds in it.
                          rye 1   raw 2
                      2. Roy made a big row when they served him raw onions and rye bread.
                          Roy 1   row 2   raw 3   rye 4
                      3. A row began after Roy said rah about the raw fish.
                          row 1   Roy 2   rah 3   raw 4

Lesson 40 Vowels sound different when used before [r] than before other consonants, so they are given special attention in this lesson. Vowels [i], [e] and [u] are longer than usual.

A.				D.						
1.	nurse	6.	thirsty	1.	D	not	nut	7.	[ᵊr]	shirt
2.	weren't	7.	possible	2.	D	cut	curt	8.	[ə]	buzz
3.	wasn't	8.	curtain	3.	S	sock	sock	9.	[ᵊr]	worm
4.	couldn't	9.	frightening	4.	D	shirt	shut	10.	[a]	sob
5.	heard	10.	exercise	5.	S	gun	gun	11.	[ᵊr]	learn
				6.	D	hurt	hot	12.	[a]	wad

Lesson 42 This is an extremely important vowel sound. Its use in reduced forms of prepositions, auxiliaries, pronouns (can, for, him, was, to, etc.) contributes heavily to the stress-timed rhythm of English.

Most of the world knows the country by the name of Burma, but recently the name has officially been changed to Myanmar.

C.			
2.	pres·i·dent	3.	com·plete·ly
4.	el·e·phant	5.	A·las·ka
6.	mu·si·cian	7.	tel·e·phone
8.	al·pha·bet	9.	pho·to·graph
10.	to·bac·co	11.	ba·na·na
12.	gas·o·line	13.	en·e·my
14.	cor·rect·ly		

D. 1. around   machine   2. Flora   florist   3. about   balloon   4. Cora   chorus

Lesson 43 **A, F, G.** The reduction of the object and possessive form of "her" [ᵊr] and the close juncture with a preceding preposition, verb, or auxiliary is the norm in speech. These are forms that most students can learn to produce to minimize their "foreign" accent.

F. 1. (take'er); stop'er, rob'er
2. kissed'er, loved'er
3. phone'er, call'er, tell'er
4. pay'er, blame'er
5. need'er, get'er, bring'er

G. 2. Do her
3. Are her
4. and her
5. Is her
6. but her

Lesson 44 **B.** (The children giggled.)
The coins jingled.
The fire crackled.
The leaves rustled.
The windows rattled.

(Ben bobbled the ball.)
The ball wobbled.
The loose handle wiggled.
The star twinkled.
He twiddled his thumbs.
The worm wiggled.

Lesson 44 **D.** Medial [d] and [t] are formed with a glottal stop accompanying the tongue position. The unstressed syllable is then simply a nasal release [n] with no vowel. It is commonly called a "syllabic "n."

Lesson 45 The small raised [ʸ] and [ʷ] indicate that the syllable containing them is shorter than those with the full vowels [iy] and [ow].

B.				E.	
1.	(Ronnie)	6.	Jimmy	1.	memo
2.	Johnny	7.	Bobby	2.	auto
3.	Archie	8.	Tommy	3.	hippo
4.	Willie	9.	Georgie	4.	typo
5.	Daddy	10.	Stevie	5.	rhino
				6.	photo

UNIT Four   Grammar Words and Intonation

Lesson 46   B. 1. 1 2 3 4 5 6 7 8 9 10 11 12 13 14 15 16 17 18 19 20

2. 10 11 12 13 14 15 16 17 18 19 20 21 22 23 24 25 26 27 28

3. 51 52 53 54 55 56 57 58 59 60 61 62 63 64 65 66 67 68 69

4. A B C D E F G H I J K L M N O P Q R S T U V W X Y Z

5. A B C D E F G H I J K L M N O P Q R S T U V W X Y Z

6. A B C D E F G H I J K L M N O P Q R S T U V W X Y Z

C. R O S E S   A R E   R E D   V I O L E T S   A R E   B L U E

S U G A R   I S   S W E E T   A N D   S O   A R E   Y O U

D. One, two, buckle your shoe.

Three, four, open the door.

Five, six, pick up sticks.

Seven, eight, shut the gate.

Nine, ten, do it again.

E, F. The teacher and the students can easily make up equations of this kind to give more practice with word grouping.

F. 1. (7 + 2) + 4
2. 10 × (3 + 7)
3. 8 + (2 × 2)
4. (1 + 9) × 3

5. 7 × (2 + 4)
6. (6 × 5) + 2
7. 3 − (5 × 5)
8. (15 − 5) × 3

G. 1. (5 + 2) × 10 = 70
2. (100 − 25) × 2 = 150
3. 5 + (6 × 5) = 35
4. (32 + 8) × 3 = 120

Lesson 47   A. 1 2 3 4 5 6 7 8 9 10 11 12 13 14 15 16 17 18 19 20

1 2 3 4 5 6 7 8 9 10 11 12 13 14 15 16 17 18 19 20

A B C D E F G H I J K L M N O P Q R S T U V W X Y Z

B. 1. b   2. f   3. c   4. e   5. a   6. d

Lesson 49   B. 1. That's your sister?

2. You didn't see her?

3. He didn't answer.

4. We weren't invited.

5. She was born in China?

6. They speak Portuguese.

7. He's a psychologist?

8. You know her?

C. Make up additional sentences and have the students reply with surprise or incredulity. This exercise also lends itself to pair work.

Lesson 50   D. 1. b   2. a   3. b   4. a

Lesson 51 B. 41 — 42   36 — 37   39 — 40   25 — 26
                93 — 94   52 — 53   65 — 66

             C. 67 — 76   28 — 82   93 — 39   52 — 25
                16 — 61   64 — 46   71 — 17

             D. 1. 18   6. 90
                2. 40   7. 50
                3. 17   8. 60
                4. 13   9. 14
                5. 15   10. 30

             E. 1. 70   2. 40   3. 14   4. 17 or 18   5. 30   6. 19   7. 18, 80

             F. 3. She was thirty.   4. He was fifty.   5. They'll be sixteen.

Lesson 52 B. Note that in two-phrase sentences, each phrase has a strong phrase stress.

Lesson 53 B. 2. seventeenth   3. third   4. twelfth   5. eightieth   6. forty-fourth

             D. 1. 1612   3. 1589   5. 1091   7. 1251
                2. 1888   4. 1390   6. 1616   8. 1519

Lesson 54 C. 1. lamps [s]   11. blouses [ᵊz]
                2. toys [z]   12. robes [z]
                3. chairs [z]   13. beds [z]
                4. shirts [s]   14. dishes [ᵊz]
                5. belts [s]   15. brooms [z]
                6. baseballs [z]   16. rings [z]
                7. watches [ᵊz]   17. birdcages [ᵊz]
                8. gloves [z]   18. clocks [s]
                9. books [s]   19. sofas [z]
               10. purses [ᵊz]   20. rugs [z]

             E. 1. tickets   6. package, letters
                2. candy   7. shirt
                3. books, shelf   8. cities
                4. stores   9. questions
                5. gift, friend   10. greetings, brother, sister

Lesson 55 C. 2. a   6. h   **D.** 1. b   4. c
                3. f   7. c   2. a   5. a
                4. g   8. j   3. b   6. c
                5. d   9. i
                        10. c

             F. 2. An artist is a painter.   **G.** lift — elevator
                3. A doctor is a physician.   lorry — truck
                4. A mistake is an error.   hoarding — billboard
                5. A chair is a seat.   bonnet — hood
                6. An auto is a car.
                7. A streetcar is a tram.
                8. A druggist is a pharmacist.

Lesson 57 See the following for the sentences that are read on tape. The teacher, of course, can vary the sentences or make up new ones to extend the practice.

             A. 1. wants [s]   11. digs [z]
                2. leaves [z]   12. cries [z]
                3. watches [ᵊz]   13. hears [z]
                4. teaches [ᵊz]   14. runs [z]
                5. rides [z]   15. closes [ᵊz]
                6. sleeps [s]   16. breathes [z]

7. sells [z]   17. smokes [s]
8. lands [ᵊz]   18. races [ᵊz]
9. sings [z]   19. comes [z]
10. laughs [s]   20. takes [s]

C. 1. The plane leaves at six o'clock.
   2. The planes land over there.
   3. The baby sleeps all the time.
   4. The children wash the dishes.
   5. The boys play baseball.
   6. Mary Ellen runs to school every day.
   7. Do you smoke a lot?
   8. Who here speaks English?

Lesson 58 B. 1. e   2. b   3. a   4. d   5. g   6. c   7. f

Lesson 59 How one pronounces the contractions *isn't, wasn't, doesn't,* and *didn't* usually identifies the speaker as a native or nonnative speaker. Practice the nasal release in class. Common errors are using no vowel [dint] for "didn't" or a full schwa instead of the nasal release: [didənt] for [didᵊnt]. It is usually helpful to explain that the tongue remains in contact with the gum ridge while air is released through the nose.

E. 1. d   5. c
   2. g   6. b
   3. a   7. f
   4. e   8. b

H. 1. Did Mr. Ames go to work today?   5. Does Tom ever walk to school?
      No, he didn't.   Yes, he does. He always does.
   2. Did it rain yesterday?   6. Who doesn't feel well?
      No, it didn't.   Mrs. Ames doesn't.
   3. Does Mary have many friends?   7. Who doesn't like girls?
      No, she doesn't.   Billy doesn't.
   4. Do Ted's sisters go to school?   8. Does Mr. Oda speak Chinese?
      No, they don't.   No, he doesn't.

UNIT Five   Consonants

Lesson 60 In this book we use regular English letters to represent all but three of the consonant phonemes in English. The three special symbols are [s̶h̶] (A̲sia); [t̶h̶] (t̲h̲ey); [ŋ] (si̲n̲g).

D. Most consonant sounds are spelled regularly. The ones whose spelling is not the same as the pronunciation symbol are these: [k] c̲ould, c̲rime; [ŋ] thin̲g̲; [t̶h̶] t̲h̲e, t̲h̲ere, t̲h̲at, wi̲t̲h̲out; [s] pla̲ce; [z] i̲s; [s̶h̶] vi̲sion.

Lesson 61 A. 1. shell 2. red   3. lake   4. mellow   5. want
            6. law   7. woven 8. lice   9. milk   10. calling

B. 2. It's a long line.   C. How does Will feel? He feels unlucky.
   3. It's a dim light.   How does Colleen feel? She feels lazy.
   4. It's a yellow pillow.   How does Mr. Lennox feel? He feels proud.
   5. It was a little lion cub.   How does Mrs. Lily feel? She feels ill.
   6. It was a lousy meal.
   8. His/Her legs are long.
   9. His tooth is loose.
   10. That fellow is lazy.
   11. The lady is tall.
   12. The lake was shallow.

Lesson 62 **A.** 1. rain   2. very   3. more   4. vow   5. wear
6. charm   7. merit   8. wave   9. bank   10. court

C. First picture: rob, robber, ring, earring, alarm, jewelry, counter
Second picture: river, race, three, arm, star, rapids, roar

Lesson 63 This fill-in reading can be completed in different ways, depending on local traffic regulations. For example, "We must pass another car on the left, never on the right," is not true everywhere. Use the differences to promote discussion, using the words "left" and "right."

A. 1. [r] carry   2. [l] low   3. [l] daily   4. [r] rain
5. [r] dairy   6. [r] bear

B. 2. It's long.   3. It's clean.   4. She's rich.   He's slow.
6. It's small.   7. It's hard.   8. He's tall.

C. right side   left side
left   right
left hand
right
left lanes   right lane
right

E. 1. lane (*b*)   2. wrong (*a*)   3. glass (*b*)   4. lock (*a*)

Lesson 64 **B.** 1. [ŋ] bang   2. [n] sin   3. [ŋ] ping   4. [n] than
5. [ŋ] singer   6. [n] thinner

E. 1. [ŋk] sink   2. [ŋ] singer   3. [ŋ] bang   4. [ŋk] banker
5. [ŋ] hanger   6. [ŋk] bunk

F. 1. sung (b)   2. singer (b)   3. hurt (a)   4. bank (a)

G. 1. some sub   sub
2. Tammy Tabby   Tabby
3. mad man   man mad
4. hung hat   hug wife
5. rigging ship   ringing bell

H. 1. comb   2. can   3. bag   4. loom   5. paid   6. long

Lesson 65 **B.** 1. [y] yell   2. [j] Jane   3. [y] yak   4. [j] jet   5. [y] yam   6. [j] jail

D. 1. jail (*a*)   2. jam (*a*)

F. 1. wine (*a*)   2. west (*b*)

H. 1. all   2. all   half   3. all   half   4. Half   half

I. 1. eat (*a*)   2. harmed (*b*)   3. hail (*b*)

Lesson 66 Voiced consonants are those in which vocal chords vibrate while producing the sound; voiceless consonants have no vibrating accompaniment. Students can feel the difference by lightly touching the vocal chord region while producing contrasting voiced/voiceless sounds such as [s] and [z]. All vowels, of course, are voiced.

A. too buy game chain van thigh zoo shock
1. Sue came   2. buy chain   3. pie thigh
4. Do Sue zoo   5. Jacques shock   6. came game van fans too

B. Point out here and in the remaining practices in the lesson that context and vowel length are often crucial in distinguishing words that differ only in having a final voiced or voiceless contrasting phoneme, as in the pairs rich/ridge; cap/cab. This is particularly important in the final unreleased consonant contrast in Part C. It does not hurt to exaggerate a bit in class to get the point across.

B. write, rider, match, matches, ridge, riches, bus, buzzing

C. back, rate, tab, hid, seat

D. 1. b   2. a   3. a

F. 2. E   3. B   4. B   5. E   6. B   7. B   8. E   9. E   10. E

G. 1. dug duck   2. paid bait   3. cab cap

Lesson 67 A fricative is a sound in which the air stream is constricted to a degree that causes friction. Typical examples are [f, v, s, z, th, th]. Voiced fricatives are fully voiced only when next to another voiced sound such as a vowel. At the beginning or end of a word, a voiced fricative is partially devoiced.

A. thirst, some, shell, van, then, seizure   **B.** 1. Thor
   1. sell   van   2. lass
   2. sell   shells   than   3. clove
   3. First   Then   4. beige
   4. thirsty   some

C. 1. [th] bathe   4. [s] mace   **D.** 1. a
   2. [v] save   5. [sh] cashier   2. a
   3. [z] maze   6. [s] gas   3. b

E. breath   teeth   teethe   mouth [th]   mouth [th]   bath bathe   breathing

Lesson 68 A stop is a sound that is formed by stopping the air stream. Examples are [t, d, ch, j]. Before a stressed vowel, a voiceless stop is aspirated (that is, accompanied by a breath of air).

B. 1. [t] bait   **B.** 1. boot (*b*)   **F.** 1. [ck] latch
   2. [th] thin   2. team(*a*)   2. [sh] sash
   3. [th] bathe   3. ladder (*b*)   3. [j] jam
   4. [th] math   4. they (*b*)   4. [sh] shin
   5. [th] they   5. [j] ledger
   6. [d] side   6. [j] agent

H. 1. a   **I.** 1. [p] flap   4. [f] cuff   **K.** 1. b
   2. a   2. [f] feel   5. [v] van   2. b
   3. a   3. [b] berry   6. [v] river   3. a
   4. a   4. b

Lesson 69 On the tape the entire table is not read—only the [r] column and the questions in Part D that relate to the words in this column. You will need to program additional practice with clusters as part of class work. Some other clusters are used by some speakers in rare or borrowed words: *pueblo, sclerosis, Vries, Sri Lanka, Zloty, Schlitz, moi*. Students can make up their own questions to be answered by words in each column.

B. 2. The opposite of very small is huge.
   3. Because the water is more pure.
   4. No, I want to make very few.
   5. I think they're very cute.
   6. They stop to look at the view.

C. 1. Duane   2. twenty   3. white   4. No, he's quiet.
   5. He swims.   6. It's square.

D. 1. Spring   2. No, some people grow them.   3. It was free.   4. brown

E. 1. blue   2. play   3. No, some people walk slow(ly).

F. 1. black   2. strong   3. travel train   4. drive
   5. throat   6. street   7. sleep dream   8. black/blue dress

G. 1. shrink   2. squeeze   3. thread   4. stranger
    5. scream   6. splinter

Lesson 70 **B.** These words are repeated.
    1. riding   2. locker   3. ringer   4. maple   5. fussy
    6. arrow   7. rival   8. etching   9. glacier

C. In informal speech the verb ending *-ing* is often pronounced [ən], in which case the words "hiding" and "Haydn" sound just the same.

C. 1. butter   2. button   3. kitten kitty, kitty
    4. redder redder   5. hiding

E. 2. smoothly   3. bravely   4. strangely/quickly
    5. clearly/frankly/softly/sharply

Lesson 71 **B.** 1. Corn is often served.   2. No, it's in the North.
    3. She should study art.   4. He cut himself with a sharp knife (or) He fell off a horse.
    5. She's wearing a scarf.   6. He or she marks them.
    7. No, that's the planet Mars.   8. The baby's name is Carl.

C. 1. The bulb is broken.   2. milk   3. gold
    4. On the shelf.   5. It's bad for my health.   6. He's Welsh.

D. 1. Camp/Go camping.   2. A month   3. It has a good lens.   4. One/An inch.
    5. Yes, I have one with red ink.   6. No, that's an ant.

UNIT Six Sentence Stress and Rhythm

Lesson 72 **D, E.** In addition to repeating and forming phrases, students can form sentences and questions using the phrases.

Lesson 73 **E.** 1. S   2. S   3. S   4. D   5. S   6. D   7. S
    8. S   9. D   10. S   11. S   12. D   13. S   14. S

H. Again we note that poems may be read with different rhythmic patterns and that your interpretation may differ from the way they are marked in the text. If your interpretation is different, give students practice with both versions. Students, too, should be given the opportunity to read the poems aloud.

Lesson 74 **C.** 2. Are they   3. Is he   4. Are you   5. Are they
    6. Are we   7. Were you   8. Was he   9. are you
    10. was she   11. Are we   12. were they

E. 2. Do you   3. Does he   4. does she   5. Does he
    6. Did they   7. did you   8. do we   9. did she

Lesson 74 **G, H, I.** The answer key supplies the questions to be used with Parts G and H, as well as the statements that are on tape for Part I. You may also vary the exercise by supplying your own questions. Part I can easily be extended and lends itself to pair work with one student making a statement and a partner responding with surprise.

G. 1. Is Bill tired? Yes, he is.
    2. Are the boys hungry? Yes, they are.
    3. Am I late? Yes, you are.
    4. Are you ready? Yes, I am.
    5. Is the water hot? Yes, it is.
    6. Is Tom thirsty? Yes, he is.
    7. Are you cold? Yes, I am.
    8. Are we early? Yes, we are.

H. 1. Do you know John? Yes, I do.
  2. Does Dorothy swim? Yes, she does.
  3. Does your sister go to school yet? Yes, she does.
  4. Do you speak some English? Yes, I do.
  5. Does it snow in Spain? Yes, it does.
  6. Do you play tennis every day? Yes, I do.

I. 3. John is sick. He is?   4. It's 6:00 o'clock. It is?
  5. The trains are late today. They are?   6. I'm leaving. You are?
  7. Tom drives a taxi. He does?   8. They speak Chinese. They do?
  9. It snows in Morocco. It does?   10. Pam plays tennis well. She does?
  11. Roberto wants to go. He does?   12. The Wilsons know Janet. They do?

Lesson 75 B. 2. their   3. our   4. my   5. your
          6. his   7. her   8. our

F. 1. his   2. your   3. their   4. her   5. our   6. our

G. 2. his   3. your   4. their   5. her
      6. my   7. our   8. your   9. her

Lesson 76 B. 2. me   3. us   4. her   5. me
          6. them   7. her   8. him

E. Insist that students say "it" with weak stress and in close juncture or liaison with the preceding verb.

Lesson 77 G. Here again, and in a few other lessons (83, 84, 88) we have examples of sentences with two phrases, each with a phrase stress. Phrases can be described in phonological terms (as well as grammatical ones) but that is beyond the scope of this book.

G. 1. e   2. g   3. a   4. f   5. d   6. h   7. b   8. c

I. The reduced form of these short prepositions is a most important factor in helping to give English its distinctive stress-timed rhythm.

J. 1. I left him at the station.
  2. The package came from Stella.
  3. He went up the stairs fast.
  4. Driver, take me to Forty-fourth Street.
  5. The letter's for Tom.
  6. He sent the gift to Helen.
  7. That's the main door of the church.
  8. I saw her in the bookstore.

Lesson 78 Linking of sounds is a complex subject, and the linking phenomena are only hinted at in this lesson. Nevertheless, practice with the examples given will provide an introduction and give useful practice with the process of linking or liaison.

Lesson 79 D. 2. Why don't you write to her?
          3. Maybe you'd better put some new batteries in it.
          4. Why don't you try using cleaning fluid on it?
          5. Why don't you ask him about it?
          6. Perhaps you'd better put some more salt in it.
          7. Perhaps you'd better get a new lock for it.
          8. I think you'll have to put some more money in it.
          9. Don't you think we'd better look for him?
          10. Why don't you try a new bulb in it?
          11. I think we'd better put a bandage on it.

F. 1. to wash today   2. to study for   3. to read   4. to do   5. to make   6. to correct

Lesson 80 **A.** In order to preserve English sentence rhythm, word stress on two-word verbs sometimes shifts back to the syllable furthest from the phrase or sentence stress.

burn up the letter (or) burn the letter up

B. a. She's hanging up clothes.
b. He's putting out a fire.
c. He's throwing away his ball.
d. She's blowing out the candles.

C. 1. I throw them away.   2. I turn the light on.
3. I take it back.   4. They give them away.
5. I clean it up.   6. I fill it out.
7. I put it up.   8. They hang them up.
9. I cut something out.   10. (It's used) to blow something up.

E. 3. We're worried about him.   7. She still isn't very good at it.
4. That isn't very convenient for us.   8. That was very helpful of you.
5. It's good for you.   9. We thought it was quite rude of her.
6. He's very fond of her.   10. She's very upset about it.

Lesson 79–81 In these few lessons we have elected to use a grammatical basis as the simplest framework to help the student understand and begin to manipulate the placement of sentence stress in sentences with both normal and contrast stress.

In addition to grammatical form, context is undoubtedly the most important factor in determining the placement of sentence stress. The introduction of a new idea or thought in a conversational exchange or reading invariably causes a shift in sentence stress to the words imparting the new information. This stress shift is ordinarily accompanied by other processes such a pronominalization, vowel reduction and ellipsis, which together reduce or downgrade the importance of other previously expressed information.

Why didn't Joe go to the dance?

He said his ex-wife was going to be there.   (new information)

Jennifer opened the box slowly and carefully.

Well, what was in it?   (new focus)

John has decided to retire this year.

Yes, his wife told me he was going to retire.   (shift of subject)

I lost my wallet yesterday.

How much money was in it?   (shift of focus)

Another factor influencing the stress placement is the tendency in English to avoid repeating the exact words of a questioner. Generally this is done by using short answers with pronouns and ellipsis. On occasion, however, the person responding does use the words of a question in full. When doing this, there is invariably a shift in sentence stress to another word and the use of low rising intonation as the end of the response. This usually shows that the listener thought the speaker (questioner) should have known the answer and perhaps asked the question for another reason.

Does she speak French?

No, she doesn't speak French.   (low rising tone at end)

What made you think she did?   (questioner should know the answer. Why do you ask?)

Are you going downtown?

Yes, I'm going downtown.   (low rising tone at end)

The need to contrast certain words or ideas also influences where the sentence stress is placed.

His sister didn't say that; his wife did.

The bee wasn't on his hat; it was in it.

Lesson 81 C. 1. c 2. d 3. a 4. e 5. b

Lesson 82 C. Sentence stress is on these words.
  2. name 3. last 4. English 5. read 6. writing
  7. my 8. Wilsons 9. don't 10. me

  D. 1. d 2. e 3. a 4. b 5. c

Lesson 83 A. 2. Oh, I thought you were going to buy an English dictionary.
  3. Oh, I thought you were going to buy a summer coat.
  4. Oh, I thought he was going to buy a yellow sweater?
  5. Oh, I thought she was going to buy a leather jacket.

  B. 2. Weaver is an English name, but Chang is a Chinese one.
  3. Children is a plural noun, but child is a singular one.
  4. Norm Bolz is a brilliant accountant, but H.R. Block is an ordinary one.
  5. South America is a large continent, but Australia is a small one.
  6. Robert Redford is a famous actor, but Harry Ames is an unknown one.

Lesson 83 C. 3. Woody Allen doesn't just act in movies. He directs them.
  4. Mr. Flaks didn't just grow the vegetables. He canned them.
  5. Ken Scott doesn't just design new dresses. He markets them.
  6. Irving Berlin didn't just write many famous songs. He sang them.
  7. Brent Hollowell doesn't just design new houses. He builds them.

Lesson 84 Most of the practice in the preceding lessons (82–84) deals with contrast stress. Emphatic stress is often marked by extra loudness and a higher pitch (pitch 4) on a particular word in a sentence.

Are shoes expensive now?

Yes, they're very expensive.

Was it a long trip?

Yes, it was much too long.

Why didn't you write a composition?

But I did write one.

Lesson 84 A. 3. Who can give it to me? 4. Who is she going with?
  5. What street is it on? 6. When will it be finished?
  7. What does he sell? 8. What did you order?
  9. Who did put it there? 10. Where was he born?

  C. 1. I don't know your brother, but I know your sister.

  2. Your brother didn't tell me that. Your sister did.

  3. I can't come, but my wife will be there.

  4. The cat wasn't in the garage. It was on the garage.

  5. I didn't tell her. I told him.

  6. The doors aren't open. The windows are.

7. The trombóne isn't a stringed instrument. The piáno is.

8. She didn't sée the thief. She héard him.

9. Your book report didn't get an A. Míne did.

10. He didn't say he cóuld come. He said he couldn't come.

11. I didn't order físh. What díd you order sir?

12. He doesn't walk for exercise. He jógs.

D. 1. It's a dentist's office.   2. His mother's taking him to the dentist.
3. It isn't on the third floor.   4. It's 401.
5. She's ringing the bell.   6. He isn't wearing a sweater.
7. She isn't wearing a suit.   8. She's carrying a book.

Lesson 84 F. We all knów the value of exercise, but does everyone dó it? We should—and not óne day a week,

but at least thrée days a week. And not for tén minutes each time but for at least thírty minutes.

And stéady exercise is much better than doing it in bits and píeces. It's also a good idea to do

different activities on different days. Swim óne day, ride a bike anóther. Walk óne time, jog the

néxt time.

And what about walking? It's the best exercise of all. However, a fást walk is better than a slów

one, but any walk is better than no walk. On súnny days you can enjoy a walk in the fresh air,

and on ráiny days you can do what a lot of people are doing—walk in a mall! But is wálking as

good as jógging or rúnning? Experts say it is. Jogging and running sómetimes cause injury to the

knee; walking séldom causes difficulty.

UNIT Seven   Final Practice and Review

B. 1. They held the rope. The thief went down the rope into the house.
2. The woman did. She was wearing it.
3. It was on the table. The thief knocked it off.
4. The woman did. She laughed when she put the jewelry in the bag. She laughed because she stole from the thief.
5. The cab was outdoors. It was waiting for her.

C. 1. her   6. your
2. you   7. its
3. him   8. and
4. our   9. she them
5. or   10. for

1. What is he doing now? Who is he working for?
2. When is her birthday? What did you get her?
3. Where did you buy them? Jane gave them to me.
4. Did you eat yet? Why don't you come along anyway?

D. 1, 3, 5, 6, and 10 are in the left column.
2, 4, 7, 8, and 9 are in the right column.

1. Twó, fóur, síx, éight,

Whó do wé appréciate?

2. Dóuble, dóuble, tóil and tróuble,

   Fíre búrn, and cáuldron búbble.

3. Rún, rún as fást as you cán,

   You cán't catch mé, I'm the gíngerbread mán.

4. How much wóod would a wóodchuck chúck,

   If a wóodchuck wóuld chuck wóod?

Self Checkup: 1. b   2. b   3. a   4. b   5. b   6. a   7. b   8. b   9. a   10. a
                   11. b   12. a   13. b   14. b   15. a   16. b   17. a   18. a   19. a   20. b

This checkup is intended only as a student learning activity. It is not a complete diagnostic or evaluative instrument.

Summary Notes

A teacher using *Sounds and Rhythm* without the cassette tapes can voice the exercises for the class. The information necessary to do this (dialogs, paragraph readings, minimal pairs, etc.) can be found in the Answer Key. The teacher should pause for students to repeat or to make other required responses. In exercises that require two voices, the teacher will have to become an actor and do both parts or find an assistant.

Before having the students work with the tapes, the teacher should ensure that students understand what they are expected to do in participatory exercises and drills, and explain any vocabulary items that the students are unlikely to know.

Many exercises should be read across the page (such as Lesson 65, Parts A, B, and C). Other exercises should be read down (Lesson 66, parts A, B, and C). Even teachers who have tapes available for laboratory use may want to voice some exercises in class this way to prepare students before using the tapes.

Students vary in background, problems, and needs, and the text can be expanded and modified to give students more practice in these areas. These are a few ways in which the text can be expanded.

1. The first part of each lesson (particularly in the vowel and consonant units) is quite short. Additional items can readily be fashioned to expand the practices as well as to repeat the material that is already there.
2. The discrimination exercises can be expanded by adding more examples.
3. Many exercises can be turned from listening or discrimination exercises into production practice by letting the students conduct the exercises themselves, either with the whole class or in pairs of students. You will need to monitor this kind of practice, of course.
4. You can adapt the final practice in many instances by changing the focus of the exercise to topics or situations that are most relevant to your students.